Psychology

Revision Notes

Author
Sheena McNamee

Series editor
Alan Brewerton

A level

EDUCATIONAL

Every effort has been made to trace copyright holders and to obtain their permission for the use of copyright material. The authors and publishers will gladly receive information enabling them to rectify any error or omission in subsequent editions.

First published 1998

Letts Educational, Schools and Colleges Division, 9–15 Aldine Street, London W12 8AW
Tel. 0181 740 2270
Fax 0181 740 2280

Text © Sheena McNamee 1998

Editorial, design and production by Hart McLeod, Cambridge

British Library Cataloguing-in-Publication Data

A CIP record for this book is available from the British Library

ISBN 1 84085 102 3

Printed and bound in Great Britain

Letts Educational is the trading name of BPP (Letts Educational) Ltd

Contents

Introduction

This book is designed to help you to organise your notes and revision – it is not intended to be a substitute for your own notes. You will notice that there is a lot of space in the margin. This is for you to put down your own ideas, explanatory notes or to add further information.

The notes have been organised following the AEB syllabus for Psychology A level. The numbering, headings and wording are taken from the syllabus. There are 8 main syllabus areas (social, comparative, bio-psychology, atypical development and abnormal behaviour, cognitive, developmental, perspectives and research methods) – you will not have studied all of them. There are 4 sub-sections within the first 6 syllabus areas (3 in perspectives and research methods). At the end of each sub-section, there are factual recall questions. You should use these during your revision to test your knowledge – the answers are in the text. The questions do not cover all the facts you need to know – it is a good idea to test yourself on other areas too – working in pairs is often a good idea.

Exam techniques

DO

- learn the Skill A and B descriptors – they tell you whether to describe or evaluate or both

- have a look at the whole paper before you start writing – this makes you less likely to miss a really good essay title

- spend a little time planning (but not too long). Jot your ideas down (key words only), then number them or put them in a logical sequence and cross them off as you do them

- read the question. Every year, many students fail to answer the questions that have been set. Take care not to latch on to one word (e.g. memory) without noticing the rest of the sentence (e.g. practical applications of ...)

- avoid pre-prepared answers. Examiners call these 'Blue Peter' answers (here's one I prepared earlier). In the exam, you will be expected to show an ability to use your knowledge in an effective way – if your answer is not specifically tailored to the question, you cannot do this

- refer to the title frequently. This helps to keep your essay focused

- refer back to other points made in your essay (impressive Skill B)

- take a watch with you – and use it! You have 45 minutes for each essay – including planning time. Don't over-run on one essay

- take care with 2 part questions – have Skill A and B been separated out? Make sure you spend an appropriate amount of time on each section – check the mark allocations. If an essay is split into two 12 mark sections, you should spend an equal amount of time on them.

DON'T PANIC

If you've done your revision, there will be essays that you can write. Try to be calm and jot down ideas for several essays. More ideas should come to you as you do this, and soon you will find that you have enough ideas to start writing on one of the topics.

Chapter one

Social psychology

1 Social cognition

1.1 Social and cultural influences upon perception

- **social perception** is the interpretation of sensory information from a social situation
- **interpretation** of sensory information is aided by past experience and expectations.

Social identity theory (SIT)

3 main theories.

- Tajfel ('82) distinguishes between personal and social identity (= **self-image**)
- **social identity** affected by groups we are members of
- categorisation important – individuals placed into social categories, e.g. gender – speeds up processing time for perception

Ingroups vs outgroups.

- an individual's group = **ingroup**, other groups are outgroups
- ingroup favouritism and outgroup bias
- outgroup members are undifferentiated = **outgroup homogeneity effect**
- SIT also stresses importance of comparison of ingroup with outgroups
- favourable comparison – positive social identity – leads to **increased self-esteem**.

Social representations

- Moscovici ('81) **social representations = beliefs shared** by members of a group, used to represent reality (what the world is like etc.)
- social representations may be shared by large or small groups of people – if large group, may be seen as 'fact' by majority of society, but flexible
- affected by social interactions such as conversations, but also by the media
- shared social representations aid communication, reduce misunderstandings
- Kruglanski ('80) lay epistemology = common knowledge – social representations, perhaps versions of scientific theory, e.g. psychoanalytic concepts
- social representations are not readily challenged – they are 'frozen' – need to be motivated in order to generate alternative theories.

Schema theory

- schemata are **internal representations of reality**, generated by experience

More rapid processing.

- schemata speed up processing of information – help to organise information, generate expectations and therefore limit the amount of information dealt with
- several categories of social schemata – **self, role, script** and **person** schemata
- schemata lead to stereotypical beliefs about groups – used to categorise, organise and generalise information – as processing is speeded up, detail about individuals in groups is ignored.

Cultural factors

- perception of a situation can be affected by cultural factors
- differing social representations lead to different interpretations of events

Interpretations of others' actions will be biased.

- e.g. Hayes ('93) Chinese girl ran away to be with Western lover – Western views supported her actions, Chinese considered her irresponsible and self-indulgent
- Western thinking is not necessarily the same as in other cultures – so Western interpretations of the actions of others will be biased and possibly incorrect
- Mbiti ('70) in many African tribes, society acts as a whole, the concept of 'self' includes the tribe – their perceptions of events will be different from a Westerner's perceptions.

1.2 Attribution theory

a. Theories of attribution

When we observe a behaviour, we infer the cause of that behaviour – we attribute a cause to it.

Loci of causality – Heider ('58)
- two loci of causality: person and situation
- **person** – internal factors caused behaviour – the individual's disposition
- **situation** – behaviour caused by external factors, e.g. lack of money.

Covariation theory – Kelley ('72)
- used to **attribute cause** to behaviour of **individuals we know**
- three variables used to infer cause as dispositional or situational:
  i. consistency, ii. consensus, iii. distinctiveness
- **dispositional** attribution likely if consistency high, consensus and distinctiveness low
- **situational** attribution likely if consistency low and distinctiveness high (consensus either)
- McArthur ('72) people do attribute cause in this way
- but – Garland et al. ('75) individuals do not choose information about three variables in order to attribute cause, only use if given it – context and personality information is preferred
- this theory requires a lot of processing of information.

Causal schemata – Kelley ('73)
- used to **attribute cause** to behaviour of **individuals we do not know**
- causal schemata = 'general conceptions a person has about how certain kinds of causes interact to produce a specific kind of effect' (Kelley ('72))
- multiple sufficient causes – several causes could be attributed to behaviour, any one would account for behaviour
- discounting principle used to narrow down possible causes if multiple sufficient causes – one may be more likely than the others
- multiple necessary causes – several factors are required to explain behaviour.

b. Errors and biases in attribution

We make predictable errors in attribution – these are attribution biases.

Fundamental attribution error (FAE)
- we tend to make dispositional attributions, even if situational is equally likely
- Ross et al. ('77) participants making up questions perceived as more knowledgeable than those answering the questions (despite unfair advantage of questioners).

Self-serving bias
- internal, dispositional attribution of cause if we are successful = **self-enhancing bias**
- external, situational attribution if we fail or make a mistake = **self-protecting bias**
- leads to increased self-esteem
- self-serving bias affects ingroup attributions also.

Actor/observer biases
- if we **observe** a behaviour we attribute a **dispositional cause** (FAE)
- if we **carry out** the same behaviour (as actor) we attribute a **situational cause**
- Jones and Nisbett ('71) more situational information available as actor
- biases affect ingroup and outgroup attribution also.

---

3 main theories for the attribution of cause.

5 main types of attribution bias.

Our social cognition is biased.

Self-handicapping – Berglas and Jones ('78)

- if we fear we may fail, tell others reason for possible failure beforehand – reasons will be situational, and therefore can be altered for next time
- **situational explanation for failure allows self-esteem to remain intact**.

Defensive attribution

- **dispositional attribution more likely if consequences are great**
- attribute cause of major disasters to individual error – we feel less anxious than if situational factors – just-world-hypothesis (Lerner ('80)).

1.3 Origins and maintenance of social and cultural stereotypes, prejudice and discrimination

Social and cultural stereotypes

- **stereotype = perception of an individual due to membership of a group rather than by individual characteristics**
- stereotypes are generated as we process social information – information is organised and put into categories, generalisations and expectations are made
- a stereotype contains generalised information about a specific group of people – they include prototypes, i.e, typical examples of groups
- stereotypes develop indirectly (through parents, the media, peers, etc.) and directly (via conditioning)
- usually based on superficial characteristics
- they develop from minimal information and are therefore distorted
- maintenance – confirmatory bias – tendency to seek and retain information that confirms stereotype, ignore information that does not fit – once formed, is difficult to change.

Prejudice and discrimination

- **prejudice is an extreme attitude** – it involves pre-judging an individual or a group
- prejudices are usually negative, but they can be positive
- attitudes have three components (usually in same direction):
  affective; cognitive; behavioural
- Allport ('54) five stages of behavioural component for racial prejudice:
  anti-locution; avoidance; discrimination; physical attack; extermination
- **discrimination = unequal treatment** of group based on prejudice – e.g. racist behaviour.

Theories of prejudice

a. Authoritarian personality – Adorno et al. ('50)

- authoritarian personality tends to be prejudiced – scores highly for authority, rigidity, intolerance, obedience and ethnocentricity
- used F(fascist)-scale to score individuals
- authoritarian personality develops if parents stress discipline, give conditional love, expect complete loyalty and obedience, ignore the needs of the child
- but – Brown ('88) cannot explain appearance of prejudice on a large scale, in a whole population – nor appearance and disappearance over time, e.g. rapid increase in Nazi Germany
- Rokeach ('60) prejudice not just linked with authoritarian (right-wing) but also extreme left-wing – dogmatic personality linked with prejudice.

b. Social identity theory (SIT)

- Tajfel ('82) positive image of social group leads to positive social identity and therefore self-image (see Chapter 1, Section 1.1)
- positive discrimination towards members of ingroup, negative towards outgroup
- distinction between groups can be arbitrary – minimal groups

We all hold stereotypical views.

Stereotypes can lead to prejudice.

Prejudice can lead to discrimination.

How does prejudice arise?

- e.g. Tajfel et al. ('71) positive discrimination to minimal ingroup members
- e.g. Sherif et al. ('61) robber's cave experiment and Elliott ('77) brown eyes, blue eyes
- but – may be culturally specific to Westerners – Wetherall ('82) Polynesian children much more generous to outgroup.

c. Scapegoat theory
- prejudice may be outlet for frustration (frustration-aggression hypothesis)
- frustrator may not be suitable target for hostility – displaced/projected onto group already have negative feelings towards (= scapegoat)
- scapegoat group often socially approved – changes over time, e.g. anti-Jewish feelings in 1930s and '40s, West Indians in '50s and '60s (England).

d. Biological explanation
- Ardrey ('66) territoriality is cause of intergroup conflicts – as found elsewhere in animal kingdom
- Dawkins ('76) kin selection – defend family – increase genes in next generation
- but – ingroups are not always family
- cannot assume animal aggression is motivated in same way as human aggression.

1.4 Reduction of prejudice and discrimination

Equal status contact

- increased contact increases likelihood of recognising similarities between groups
- if meet individuals, lessens outgroup homogeneity effect
- Aronson ('80) stereotypes reinforced if contact is of unequal status
- Deutsch and Collins ('51) integrated housing (equal status) did reduce prejudice, segregation increased
- e.g. Minard ('52) black and white miners not prejudiced at work (equals), were when above ground – do not generalise to all situations
- may not generalise to all members of group
- desegregation of US schools did not increase contact between groups greatly – groups stick together – Stephan ('78) black children became more prejudiced towards white.

Pursuit of common (superordinate) goals
- Aronson et al. ('78) jigsaw classroom technique – members of inter-racial group interdependent – did reduce prejudice (and increase self-esteem and academic performance)
- but – did not generalise to other members of race, only liked specific individuals
- Sherif et al. ('61) robber's cave – co-operation on task reduced intergroup prejudice – but only if goal achieved.

Teaching
- Elliott ('90) brown eyes, blue eyes children were followed up – less prejudiced and more tolerant
- Cook ('78) states five factors for reduction of prejudice: equal-status; co-operation between groups; exposure to non-stereotypical individuals; personal acquaintance; environmental support.

Problems for methods of reducing prejudice and discrimination:

- formation of stereotypes in unconscious and integral part of social cognition
- prejudices allow increased personal benefit of high self-esteem – difficult to remove
- stereotypes and therefore prejudices are resistant to change – confirmatory bias
- lack of generalisation to whole group or other situations (see above).

Section 1

1. What are the main explanations for social perception?
2. Describe four aspects of social identity theory.
3. What is a social representation?
4. What factors can influence social representations?
5. What is a schema?
6. How do schemata aid social cognition?
7. How can culture affect social perception?
8. What are the main explanations for attribution?
9. In the covariation theory, which three variables are used to infer cause?
10. What evidence is there to suggest the covariation theory is correct?
11. What are the main problems with the covariation theory?
12. Describe the main aspects of the causal schemata theory of attribution.
13. What is an attribution bias?
14. List the main types of attribution bias.
15. Explain the fundamental attribution error.
16. What is a stereotype?
17. How are stereotypes generated and maintained?
18. Define prejudice and discrimination.
19. List the main theories of prejudice.
20. Provide evidence for and against the SIT theory of prejudice.
21. List the main factors that can lead to reduction of prejudice (don't forget Cook ('78)).
22. What evidence is there to suggest that equal status contact reduces prejudice?
23. What evidence indicates that cooperation on a task reduces prejudice?
24. What are the main problems for reduction of prejudice?

2 | Social relationships

2.1 Theories of interpersonal relationships

Economic theories
Economic theories explain relationships in terms of cost-benefit analysis for individuals.

a. Exchange theory – Thibaut and Kelley (1959)
- **satisfaction in relationship is measured in terms of profit**
- CL (comparison level) = average level of rewards and costs, used to compare relationships
- if current ratio > CL, satisfied with relationship – if current < CL, dissatisfied
- CL_{ALT} (comparison level for alternatives) = level perceived in alternative relationship

- if CL_{ALT} > current ratio, should end current relationship and seek alternative
- four stages in forming relationship: sampling; bargaining; commitment; institutionalisation.

b. Equity theory – Adams (1965)
- equity means an individual **gets out what they put in** (i.e. not equality) – effort = gain
- if effort > gain, leads to anger and dissatisfaction with relationship
- if gain > effort, leads to guilt and dissatisfaction (lesser extent than if losing)
- may stay in inequitable relationship if fear of losing investment (Rusbult ('83)).

For	Against
• some research supports – e.g. calculation of what is owed can occur	• research is contrived, lacks ecological validity
• explains why stay in unhappy relationship – CL_{ALT} low (no alternatives)	• Rubin ('73) capitalistic theory, ignores behaviours with no expectation of reward
	• Mills and Clark ('80) 2 types of couple – exchange and communal

Need satisfaction – Argyle (1994)
- **relationships satisfy seven social needs/motives**: biological needs; dependence; affiliation; dominance; sex; aggression; self-esteem.

For	Against
• many relationships do satisfy many of these needs	• selfish, one-sided explanation – ignores giving behaviours

Reinforcement-affect model – Byrne and Clore (1970)
- **we like those that reward us and dislike those that punish us**
- we associate individuals with good/bad feelings (affect) via conditioning.

For	Against
• Veitch and Griffitt ('76) feelings toward stranger affected by situation when met (good/bad news)	• Aronson and Mills ('59) pleasant experience with group did not lead to more positive feelings

Socio-biological theory – Wilson (1986)
Evolutionary explanation.
- interpersonal relationships provide a **survival advantage** – adaptive behaviour
- women should choose good providers as mates and try to keep them
- men should maximise reproductive output by mating with as many women as possible.

For	Against
• Dunbar ('95) lonely hearts ads – women seek resources, men offer – opposite with attractiveness	• only reproductive relationships explained
	• generalisation from animal behaviour
	• legitimises gender stereotypical behaviours

General problems with theories of relationships

- studies investigate behaviour of American college students – **not representative sample**
- research mostly **ignores** homosexual relationships, friendships, extra-marital relationships
- **cross-cultural studies have found differences in relationships** – North American model and theories not universal – see below (Section 2.4)
- research is **artificial** and subject to effects of memory, misinterpretation, social role expectations
- Duck and Sants ('83) tend to be **static** – ignore changes occurring in relationships over time
- difficulty measuring quality of relationship.

Is relationship research valid and reliable?

2.2 Formation, maintenance and dissolution of interpersonal relationships

a. Formation
There are a number of factors involved in our attraction to, and relationship formation with, others.

7 factors in the formation of relationships.

i. physical attractiveness – attractive seen as 'good' = Halo effect, e.g. Dion ('72)
- matching hypothesis – partners of similar attractiveness, e.g. Murstein ('71) showed this with married couples, e.g. Silverman ('71) observational study
- but – Walster et al. ('66) 'computer dance' did not support matching

ii. similarity – attracted to those similar to us
- Rubin ('73) similarity is rewarding – joint activities possible, agreement so increased self-esteem, easier to communicate, similar will like us
- Hill et al. ('76) more similar more likely to stay together
- Kerchoff and Davis ('62) similarity important early in relationship, complementarity in long-term

iii. complementarity – attracted to opposites? – those whose attributes complement our own
- Winch ('58) partner's strengths should compensate for own weaknesses, e.g. dominant–submissive, nurturant–receptive

iv. proximity – more likely to encounter those in close proximity – field of availables Kerchoff ('74) – form relationships with those we encounter
- Festinger et al. ('50) university campus – near stairs have more friends (more encounters)
- Argyle ('81) more interactions, more polarised attitudes (usually, but not always, positive)

v. familiarity – prefer familiar – Zajonc et al. ('74) more positive evaluation of photographs seen more often, also for music, paintings, political candidates
- may be because familiar is predictable and does not induce anxiety

vi. reciprocal liking – we like those who like us
- Backman and Secord ('59) told participants that individuals would like them, participants sought these individuals in group work
- Aronson ('76) like individual most if initially negative, then positive towards us (gain)
- but – Byrne and Rhamey ('65) ingratiation effect and Hewitt ('72) extra credit effect

vii. perceived competence – we like those who are competent
- but – Aronson et al. ('66) most liked is intelligent (competent) but clumsy (fallible)

b. Maintenance
- Dindia and Baxter ('87) maintenance and repair strategies
- **maintenance** – important for maintaining contact and preventing problems from arising
- **repair** – used when problems arise, involve analysis of relationship
- newly-weds use more maintenance strategies than those married for longer
- **social penetration theory** – Altman and Taylor ('73) gradual self-disclosure, reveal more about self – Rubin ('75) must be same for both partners = norm of reciprocity.

Once formed, relationships must be maintained...

c. Dissolution
- **equity theory** – lack of equity – gain or loss results in dissatisfaction with relationship
- **social exchange theory** – if CL_{ALT} > current ratio, leave current relationship
- **social penetration theory** – imbalance in self-disclosure – too much/little
- Duck ('81) two types of cause of breakdown: **personal** and **precipitating** (situational) factors
- Duck ('88) three factors in breakdown process:
  - **i. antecedents** – e.g. youth, low SES, different backgrounds, divorced parents
  - **ii. specific causes** – lack of self-expression, rule breaking, deception, boredom, relocation
  - **iii. stages – four phases:** intra-psychic; dyadic; social; grave-dressing.

... or they dissolve.

2.3 Components of interpersonal relationships

Goals and conflicts
- Argyle et al. ('81) three major goals: **physical well-being**; **social acceptance**; **task goals**
- relationships may break down if partners have different goals
- Argyle and Furnham ('83) 3 main factors associated with satisfaction in relationships: **common interests**; **social and emotional support**; **material and instrumental help**
- spouse is major source of conflict and satisfaction.

4 main components of interpersonal relationships.

Rules
- Argyle and Henderson ('85) several types of rules, including: **intimacy** rules; **rewardingness**; **coordination** and avoiding difficulties; **behaviour with third parties**   *some cultural variation*
- some rules are universal and general (e.g. respecting privacy), others may depend on culture, situation and relationship
- 2 main functions of rules: regulatory and reward.

Power and roles
- **power is the ability to influence another's behaviour**   *gender effects*
- **social roles are expected behaviours** in specific situations
- social roles and power are important aspects of relationships – stereotypical roles involve passivity and nurturance in women, dominance in men
- e.g. Gavey ('92) showed coercive power men have over women in sexual relationships.

Investigated using discourse analysis.

Activities
- different activities important in different relationships – important activities are not necessarily most common ones   *gender effects*
- Nardi ('92) gender differences in same-sex relationships – women more expressive
- Segal ('90) men's relationships may be affected by fear of appearing homosexual.

2.4 Individual, social and cultural variations

Individual differences
- **gender differences** – women's same-sex relationships are more expressive (Nardi ('92))

- Argyle and Henderson ('84) affection and emotional support more likely in females' relationships
- Latane and Bidwell ('77) women tend to affiliate more in public
- **age has little effect**, though privacy is more valued with age (Argyle and Henderson ('84))
- individuals have different **needs for affiliation** – some need more positive stimulation and attention than others (Hill ('87)).

Social and cultural differences

Western relationships seen as "normal".

- Argyle et al. ('85) **friendship rules** in different cultures – some **universal** rules (e.g. respect privacy), others **culture-specific** (e.g. Japanese – many rules to avoid conflict)
- Moghaddam et al. ('93) **Western social relationships** = individualistic, temporary and voluntary, **non-western** = collective, permanent and obligatory
- much of research is probably irrelevant for explanation of non-western relationships
- Yelsma and Athappilly ('88) higher satisfaction in arranged marriages
- most research is carried out by Western researchers, results give Western viewpoint.

2.5 Effects of relationships

Happiness

Relationships are associated with a number of positive factors.

- Argyle ('92) happiness has 2 components: positive emotions and positive states of mind
- **positive emotions** – generated by sharing enjoyable experiences, synchrony and coordination
- **positive states of mind** – contentment, satisfaction with job/life
- Veroff et al. ('81) higher % of married are 'very happy'
- very few studies on cohabitation to compare with.

Mental health

Correlation studies.

- **marital status is linked to mental health** – Cochrane ('88) divorced most likely to be admitted to mental hospital, married least likely (gender differences, though)
- Argyle and Henderson ('85) divorced/separated most likely mentally ill
- Cowen et al. ('73) lack of friends in childhood associated with later mental illness.

Social support

- when anxious, people prefer to wait with others (Schachter ('59))
- Kamarck et al. ('90) lowered response to stressor when with friend
- Argyle ('92) **buffering hypothesis** – social support buffers from stress – enhances self-esteem, positive regard leads to positive emotions, discussing and sharing problems.

Need fulfilment

- Schachter ('59) social isolation has dramatic negative effects, cannot be sustained for long – **social interaction is a basic human need**.

Self-development

- **looking-glass self** (see Chapter 6, Section 3) – image of self develops through others' responses to us – positive interactions lead to positive self-image and high self-esteem
- **social comparison** – interactions with others allow us to compare ourselves to them
- **development of relationships** – practice at interactions develops our social skills, allowing more complex interactions in future.

Section 2

1. What are the main theories of interpersonal relationships?

2. What are the main problems for both economic theories of interpersonal relationships?

3. What is the reinforcement-affect model?

4. Give one piece of evidence for and against the reinforcement-affect model.

5. What are the main assumptions of the socio-biological theory of interpersonal relationships?

6. What are the problems of the socio-biological theory?

7. Give 4 general problems with the theories of relationships.

8. List the possible factors involved in formation of a relationship.

9. Give 1 piece of evidence to suggest that proximity is an important factor.

10. What are the maintenance and repair strategies of Dindia and Baxter ('87)?

11. How does social penetration theory explain maintenance of relationships?

12. How do the 2 economic theories explain relationship breakdown?

13. How does social penetration theory explain the dissolution of relationships?

14. What are Duck's stages of breakdown?

15. List the main components of interpersonal relationships.

16. What goals are associated with relationships?

17. What rules are associated with relationships?

18. In what ways does gender affect relationships?

19. Give an example of a universal and a culture-specific rule.

20. How do western and non-western relationships differ?

21. What problems arise for research into relationships due to cultural differences?

22. What are the main effects of relationships?

23. What evidence is there to suggest that social support is an effect of relationships?

3 | Social influence

3.1 Conformity, obedience and independent behaviour

a. Conformity

- **conformity = 'a change in a person's behaviour or opinion as a result of a real or imagined pressure from a group of people'** (Aronson ('76))
- direct or deliberate pressure is not required by the group (majority or minority)
- 3 main studies: Sherif ('35), Asch ('52) and Zimbardo et al. ('73).

Sherif (1935)
autokinetic effect = ambiguous task – in groups, estimates converge
- conformity was unconscious
- others in group used for informational social influence in ambiguous situation

Asch (1952)

line comparison – not ambiguous, obvious correct answer, 74% participants conformed to incorrect answer of stooges at least once (overall 32% trials conformed)

* reasons: i. few said **perceptual distortion**; ii. **distortion of judgement** = private change; iii. **distortion of action** = public compliance.

Variations

* **max. conformity** if at least three confederates, Latane and Wolf ('81) increases with group size
* **more conformity** with high status confederates, or more difficult tasks
* **less conformity** if dissenter in group, or if written answers
* still **some conformity** if not face-to-face – e.g. Crutchfield ('55) military personnel.

Zimbardo et al. (1973)

Stanford Prison Study – 25 men allocated randomly to be prisoners and guards – guards and prisoners conformed to roles given – stopped after 6 days – guards aggressive, prisoners depressed

* **conformity** to social role = **normative influence** of group
* reflective sunglasses of guards, prisoner numbers – **deindividuation**.

Evaluation

* people evidently do conform and level of conformity depends on situation
* other studies have shown **differences in levels of conformity** – e.g. Milgram ('61) French conform less than Norwegians – Larsen ('74) replicated Asch study in US, lower conformity rates – Perrin and Spencer ('80) lower in UK – **NB** dates of studies vary
* Kelman ('58) **two types of conformity**:
  i. **compliance** (outward agreement only); ii. **internalisation** (internal change)
* **ethics** – deception, anxiety, severe suffering in Zimbardo's study
* **conformity is not necessarily a negative trait** – conformity is required for an ordered society.

b. Obedience

* **obedience = following orders** – does not imply any change in opinion
* most important study is by Milgram ('63)
* 65% participants gave full 450V, even though learner's screams had stopped at 270V.

Variations

* no verbal feedback from 'learner' = 100% obedience to 450V
* **proximity of learner** (closer decreases), **proximity of experimenter** (increases)
* **status of experimenter and location** (low status decreases)
* **no gender differences** (but Kilham and Mann ('74) Australia, less in females)
* Smith and Bond ('93) varies in different countries – cultural differences or poor replication?
* explanation for obedience: Milgram's **agentic theory** – 2 levels of functioning:
  autonomous = individual, voluntary actions, include responsibility
  agentic = agent of another/others – not responsible for actions – trained as children to obey
* also, demand characteristics of experiment, e.g. agreed to cooperate, must be safe
* sequential nature of shocks – small increments – little incentive to stop at any point.

Evaluation

* Milgram's work criticised on several counts – lack of ecological validity, ethics (deception, anxiety) – though debriefing and follow-up questionnaire sent out
* replication – other research backs up high levels of obedience, though actual % varies
* supported by Hofling et al. ('66) field study with nurses.

Conformity occurs in a variety of situations, for a variety of reasons.

Culture affects conformity.

Levels of obedience vary depending on the situation.

c. Independent behaviour

Non-conformers or disobedient participants are showing independent behaviour.

Anti-conformist behaviour is not independent since it relies on a conforming group to oppose – it does not require an individual to generate their own opinions.

- not all individuals conform or obey – Asch's study showed independent behaviour in 68% trials, 26% individuals never conformed – Milgram's study 35% independence
- many factors affect the likelihood of independent behaviour – any factors which reduce conformity/obedience/increase independent behaviour (see above)
- Milgram ('73) disobedient models increase participants' independence
- education about danger of blind obedience increases independence
- individual differences – Burger ('92) individuals with a high need for control show more independent behaviour – Crutchfield ('55) independence linked with self-reliance, intelligence and leadership ability
- Asch noted 3 types of independent behaviour: **confidence** in own perception; **withdrawal**; **tension** and **doubt**.

3.2 Social power

Social power – ability to influence behaviour of others
- French and Raven ('60) five types of group power: **reward**; **expert**; **informational**; **coercive**; **referent**
- **normative influence** leads to compliance, e.g. coercive, reward, referent power
- **informational influence** leads to internalisation, e.g. informational, expert power
- Schriesheim et al. ('91) two categories of social power: position and personal power.

Leadership

Leadership qualities
- early work suggested leaders' personalities were not different, e.g. Mann ('59)
- Kirkpatrick and Locke ('91) identified several characteristics of successful business leaders: **flexibility**; **drive**; **self-confidence**; **cognitive ability**; **honesty and integrity**; **creativity**.

Are leaders special?

Leadership style
- Roethlisberger and Dickson ('39) **production oriented and interpersonally oriented**
- Bales and Slater ('55) **task-specialist and social-emotional specialist** – different leader type suitable in different situations, may be two leaders complementing each other
- Lewin et al. ('39) **authoritarian, democratic and laissez-faire** leadership styles – democratic produced best quality work
- Weiss and Friedrichs ('86) democratic basketball coaches produced more successful players
- democratic is not necessarily the best style in all situations, though.

Democratic is not necessarily the best style in all situations.

Fiedler's contingency theory ('78)
- task/relationship centred leader suited to different situations
- used LPC (least preferred co-worker) scale to rate individuals
- three factors affect favourability of situation:
  relationship between leader and followers; how **structured** task is; **power** leader exerts
- low LPC best in favourable and unfavourable situations, high LPC best in moderate.

Vroom's decision-making model ('84)
- decision-making situations have a number of characteristics including: **time pressure**, **information** available, **likelihood of acceptance** by subordinates, **importance of acceptance**

- different styles are effective in different situations – **autocratic**, **consultative**, **based on group decision**
- the leader should alter style depending on the type of decision-making situation
- but – subordinates preference is for participation in all situations (Field and House ('90)).

Does the situation make the leader?

Situation dependent approach
- Fireston et al. ('75) groups choose leader with appropriate qualities for task – not always same individual
- Lorzetta ('55) aggressive leaders emerged in time-pressured groups, not in control groups.

Expectations
- McGregor ('60) two management beliefs: **Theory X** = workers are lazy, **Theory Y** = workers work hard if appreciated
- self-fulfilling prophecy – if leaders subscribe to Theory Y this is how their workers behave
- House ('71) **path-goal theory** of leadership – incorporated self-fulfilling prophecy – good leader should respect workers and allow to achieve personal goals.

Transformational/charismatic leaders (Greenberg and Baron (1995))
- followers of transformational leaders work exceptionally hard
- these leaders have particular qualities: **vision**, **a plan** to achieve vision, they **justify their actions**, they have excellent **communication skills**, **confidence** in self and followers, they are **risk takers**.

Followership
- followers respond best when respected and treated as responsible adults (path-goal theory)
- Lewin et al. ('39) suggests best work for democratic leader
- followers prefer to participate in decision-making process, even when Vroom's theory suggests they do not need to
- followers affect leaders' expectations, and therefore future follower behaviour
- Adorno et al. ('50) authoritarian personalities are more obedient
- Greenberg and Baron ('95) followers of transformational leaders show enthusiasm for, and high levels of loyalty to, their leader, work harder than expected and sacrifice personal goals.

3.3 Collective behaviour

Types of crowd – Brown ('65)
- **acquisitive**; **escaping**; **expressive**; **aggressive**.

Peaceful crowds
- generally, crowds are peaceful
- Benewick and Holton ('87) open air mass, interviews, sense of **crowd unity** and **sharing**.

Non-peaceful crowds
- occasionally crowds become disorderly, sometimes riot
- Le Bon (1895) – **mob psychology** – crowd reverted to **animal state**, **lack of reasoning** and rational thought – **unity** of mob
- Zimbardo ('69) explains using **deindividuation** – **loss of personal identity, anonymity**
- Diener ('79) deindividuation leads to five outcomes:
  normal behavioural restraints weakened
  heightened sensitivity to emotional states

Violent behaviour in crowds.

inability to monitor and regulate behaviour
lower concern for social approval
lower capacity for rational planning
- Banyard ('89) police belief in crowd as irrational mob may have increased casualties at Hillsborough – did not try to explain what was going on.

Why do peaceful crowds become violent?
- Smelser ('62) long-term perception of grievances needed
- Waddington et al. ('87) noted 'flashpoints' in political demonstrations, generated recommendations for keeping crowd peaceful – reduces grievances:
  1. **liaison** between police and organisers
  2. **self-policing** as far as possible
  3. **minimum of force** by police
  4. **communication skills** in crowd managers
  5. police should be **accountable** for actions
- also, six levels of analysis of crowd violence: **structural**; **political/ideological**; **cultural**; **contextual**; **spatial**; **interactional** – no single factor is enough to produce disorder.

Additional information
- the presence of others can affect us in other ways, e.g. **social facilitation** (we work harder), **social inhibition** (we perform less well), **decision-making becomes polarised**, **bystander apathy** (see Section 4.1).

Can we reduce crowd violence?

Questions

Test yourself – then check your answers.

Section 3

1. What is conformity?

2. What are the three important studies of conformity?

3. What are the two types of conformity (Kelman ('58))?

4. What are the explanations for conformity in Sherif, Asch and Zimbardo's studies?

5. What factors can affect the level of conformity?

6. What are the findings of Milgram's original study into obedience?

7. What factors can affect the level of obedience?

8. What ethical problems arise in studies of conformity and obedience?

9. What factors increase the likelihood of independent behaviour?

10. List the types of group power and their effects.

11. Leaders are different. What evidence suggests this is the case?

12. What are the types of leadership style?

13. Explain Vroom's decision-making model ('84).

14. What evidence is there to suggest situation dependence in leadership?

15. What factors affect follower behaviour?

16. Explain what is meant by 'mob psychology'.

17. How does Zimbardo explain mob behaviour?

18. How can crowd violence be reduced?

4 | Pro- and anti-social behaviour

4.1 Altruism and bystander behaviour

Pro-social behaviour
- **pro-social behaviour** involves aiding others; altruism and helping behaviour are pro-social
- **altruism** = helping performed at cost to individual helping, no expectation of reward
- **helping behaviour** = giving assistance, not necessarily with a cost to the helper.

Bystander behaviour

Why do we choose to help – or not?

- originally referred to as bystander apathy – why do bystanders choose to help/not? – often choose not to, e.g. Kitty Genovese case
- several factors affect likelihood of helping:
  i. **pluralistic ignorance** – e.g. Latane and Darley ('68) smoke-filled room
  ii. **diffusion of responsibility** – bigger group, less individual responsibility to react
  iii. **audience inhibition** – we do not want to look potentially foolish in front of others
  iv. **competence** – more likely to help if have skills useful in situation – Cramer et al. ('88) nurses more likely to help than students if other bystanders
  v. **characteristics of bystander** – Bierhoff et al. ('91) helpers had high internal locus of control, felt socially responsible, believed in 'just world'
  vi. **characteristics of victim** – Piliavin et al. ('81) more likely to help those appearing weak, sober, similar to us, physically attractive than drunk, unkempt or unattractive
  vii. **location** – more helping in rural areas.

Explanations of pro-social behaviour
There are several explanations of pro-social behaviour – some cannot explain truly selfless behaviour, but would argue that no behaviour is truly selfless.

Helping another is a cost to ourselves – so why do we do it?

- **natural selection** – selfish gene – apparent altruism – only altruistic at level of individual – beneficial to gene pool, inclusive fitness increased by 'altruistic' behaviour (Chapter 2, Section 3.1)
- **learning theory** – pro-social behaviour is rewarded and therefore repeated
- **normative explanations** – social norms followed, e.g. Gouldner ('60) reciprocity norm (help those who help us), Berkowitz and Daniels ('63) social responsibility norm (help those relying on us)
- **negative-state relief model** – Cialdini et al. ('87) helping others reduces our anxiety (negative state), motivates us to help
- **empathy-altruism model** – Batson et al. ('81) we empathise with individual in need and distressed, so help them – innate mechanism
- **empathy-joy model** – Smith et al. ('89) helping makes us feel good
- **decision model** – Latane and Darley ('70) – cognitive model – helping depends on a number of sequential factors, each factor increases likelihood of help: noticing event, defining as emergency, assuming responsibility, knowing type of help needed, implementing decision
- **cost-benefit model** – Piliavin et al. ('81) help if benefits outweigh costs – benefits include increased self-esteem, social approval – costs include time, effort, risk of harm.

4.2 Social-psychological theories of aggression

- **anti-social behaviour** is behaviour which is intended to harm another
- subdivisions of aggression: **hostile** (aim to harm another); **instrumental** (harm is not aim)
- Maslow ('68) **natural aggression** (e.g. self-defence) and **pathological aggression** (violence).

4 social – psychological theories.

Social learning theory
- **observation, imitation** of model and **reinforcement** important
- rewarded behaviours are more likely to be repeated – **positive reinforcement**
- **vicarious learning** – learning from observing others being rewarded/punished
- Bandura et al. ('63) children will imitate aggressive behaviour directed at Bobo doll
- more imitation if: model rewarded; model of same sex as child; model exhibiting sex-appropriate behaviour; model is highly regarded or powerful
- less imitation if model punished – but still learnt behaviour since show it if rewarded for it
- **problems** – unusual situation with demand characteristics – ethical considerations.

Frustration-aggression hypothesis
- Dollard et al. ('39) frustration due to inability to reach goals leads to aggressive behaviour – motivation energies redirected to aggressive behaviour
- Buss ('61) frustrated participants gave victims more 'electric shocks'
- Berkowitz ('62) frustration and external trigger/cue are required for aggressive behaviour
- **problems** – frustration can lead to passivity, not aggression (Seligman ('75) learned helplessness) – aggression can occur without frustration (e.g. boxing).

Response to environment
More aggression in hot, noisy, smoky, smelly, crowded places!

- **environmental factors** can lead to aggressive behaviour
- Donnerstein and Wilson ('76) more aggression in noisy situations
- Baron and Bell ('74) more aggressive behaviour between 81° and 85°F
- Aiello et al. ('79) more aggressive and competitive in crowded space
- Zillman ('79) explanation – environmental factors heighten arousal.

Individual factors
- **type A behaviour** (impatience, competitiveness etc.) is associated with aggression – relate to frustration-aggression – Type A more likely to be frustrated (Kanner et al. ('81))
- **attribution of cause** of another's action affects aggression (Kremer and Stephens ('83))
- **gender differences** – males more likely to be physically aggressive, females at least equally likely to be indirectly aggressive – may be social learning or testosterone levels
- Zillman ('83) **excitation transfer theory** – increased arousal, transfer to aggressive act.

4.3 Reduction and control of aggressive behaviour

Reduction of aggressive behaviour in crowds
- set of recommendations by Waddington et al. ('87) – see Section 3.3.

Reduction of individual aggressive behaviour

Social learning theory
- use reinforcement of non-aggressive behaviours and punishment of aggressive behaviours – non-aggressive models should be provided, e.g. on TV.
- Bower and Hilgard ('81) punishment can be effective if it is predictable, prompt and intense
- non-aggressive punishment – aggressive behaviour can be reinforced by attention.

Freud ('20) – catharsis
- **catharsis = discharge of built up aggression** (unconscious drive) – can channel into physical activities, e.g. sport, so less likely to show aggressive behaviour
- but – many activities do not reduce aggressive behaviour, e.g. Arms et al. ('80) attending competitive events increases aggression.

Incompatible responses
- cannot have 2 incompatible emotions simultaneously – generate happiness or empathy in angry individual, less likely to be aggressive.

Social skills training
- better social skills, less frustration, less aggression (Toch ('85)) – Schneider ('91) training reduced aggressive behaviour in children.

Psychosurgery
- lobotomy – once popular, very rarely used now and not for aggressive behaviour – many additional effects.

Several different approaches to reducing aggression.

4.4 Media influences on pro- and anti-social behaviour

- **media = TV, video, film, radio, books, magazines, newspapers, comics, computers**
- most studies investigate TV and film, and investigate links with anti-social behaviour
- Bandura ('65) showed that children will imitate behaviour seen on film.

Anti-social behaviour
- Cumberbatch ('87) proportion of programmes containing violence decreased since 1970s, but no. of violent acts per hour has increased on violent programmes
- many more channels are now available – do not have to follow 9pm watershed.

Many studies have investigated effects of TV violence:
- Parke et al. ('77) juvenile delinquents exposed to violent programmes increased aggression on some measures – but – not random groups, most effect on already violent individuals
- Berkowitz ('69) more electric shocks given if seen aggressive film
- Milavsky et al. ('82) small correlations between viewing and aggression, but family background more highly correlated
- Williams ('86) introduction of TV associated with increase in aggressive behaviour for boys and girls, all ages studied
- but – children are not passive observers – have past experience, opinions of their own
- **nb** – violence on TV can be counteracted – Eron et al. ('83) teaching children that TV violence is not real life etc. linked with less aggression, and more pro-social behaviours.

Links between TV and violence.

Specific effects of TV violence
- **arousal** – watching violence on TV increases arousal levels – Zillman ('83) excitation transfer theory, can transfer arousal to aggressive behaviour (see above)
- **disinhibition** – provide norms of behaviour, aggressive behaviour seen as acceptable
- **imitation** – vicarious reinforcement, modelling – learn behaviours seen on TV
- **desensitisation** – repeated viewing of violence leads to reduction in emotional response, violence more easily tolerated.

Pro-social behaviour
- TV can provide positive social norms as well as negative ones
- Stein and Friedrich ('72) 4 weeks of pro-social TV, more likely to show pro-social behaviour
- Baran ('79) more helping behaviour if watched 'helping' episode of 'The Waltons'
- Forge and Phemister ('87) watching 'Sesame Street' associated with pro-social behaviour.

Pro-social behaviour will be imitated.

Don't forget – TV can have a positive influence.

TV can provide other useful functions:
- Messenger-Davies ('89) ideas for play; common interest with family/friends
- Gunter and McAleer ('90) education, entertainment and peer contact.

4.5 Cultural diversity in pro- and anti-social behaviour

Pro-social behaviour
- levels of pro-social behaviour vary greatly
- Whiting and Whiting ('75) 8% American, 100% Kenyan children showed altruism
- Eisenberg and Mussen ('89) children on kibbutz more cooperative
- may be due to social learning theory, differing social norms, child-rearing practices.

Anti-social behaviour
- Scott ('92) murder rates per 100,000 population vary enormously, e.g. 0.9 Norway, 1.4 Britain, 9.9 USA, 683 New Guinea
- cultural differences in attitudes towards aggression – Osterwell and Nagano-Hakamural ('92) Japanese express within family, Israeli express outside
- Mead ('35) Arapesh (New Guinea tribe) boys and girls encouraged to be non-aggressive.

Groups within a culture (microcultures) may have different attitudes to aggression – Kaufman et al. ('90) minority Hispanics more moody, minority Anglos more aggressive at school.

Questions

Section 4

1. Define altruism, pro-social behaviour and helping.

2. What factors affect bystander behaviour?

3. Give 3 studies into bystander behaviour, and their findings.

4. List the explanations of pro-social behaviour.

5. Explain the sub-divisions of the term aggression?

6. What are the main social-psychological theories of aggression?

7. What are the main assumptions of the social-learning theory?

8. Provide evidence for and against the frustration-aggression hypothesis.

9. What environmental factors have an effect on aggressive behaviour?

10. What individual factors have an effect on aggressive behaviour?

11. List the methods for reduction of aggressive behaviour.

12. Explain how social learning theory would be used to reduce aggression.

13. What evidence is there to suggest that watching TV and aggression are linked?

14. What are the specific effects of TV violence?

15. What useful functions can TV serve?

16. Give examples of cultural variation in pro-social behaviour.

17. Give examples of cultural variation in anti-social behaviour.

Comparative psychology

1 Evolutionary determinants of behaviour

1.1 Evolutionary concepts as explanations of behaviour

What is evolution?
- evolution occurs via a process called **natural selection**
- individuals of a species vary genetically and show different characteristics
- those individuals with most suitable characteristics (best adapted) are most likely to survive and reproduce (**survival of the fittest**)
- those individuals reproducing the most pass on most genes to the next generation.
- offspring have similar genes and therefore characteristics to their parents
- an individual's fitness depends on the number of offspring produced
- **selection pressure** = pressure exerted so that only some (fittest) survive
- **evolution is a gradual process**, with small changes occurring from generation to generation – over many generations, large changes can occur.

This is vital – it will be used to explain many behaviours throughout this section.

Evaluation of evolution
- **fossil record** shows organisms have evolved over time
- **artificial selection** shows how the mechanism works
- **natural experiments** have shown changes in populations after changes in the environment
- but – cannot prove cause and effect from fossil record and natural experiments.

Evolution does occur.

Evolution as an explanation for non-human animal behaviours
- **natural selection** can only affect **behaviours that have genetic components**
- **innate behaviours** can be recognised as **species-specific**, all individuals show behaviour, stereotyped and same every time, produced in response to sign stimulus
- some behaviours have **innate components** but are **modified by experience**
- those individuals showing adaptive behaviour are selected for, over time, behaviours can evolve in the same way as physical features.

Evolution can explain a wide variety of behaviours.

Examples
- **signalling** behaviours have evolved (see Section 3.4) including **courtship** and **aggression**
- evolutionary concepts can explain **mating strategies**, **parental investment** and **conflict with offspring** (see Sections 2.1–4)
- evolution suggests individuals should be selfish – maximise reproductive output – but altruism occurs in animal behaviour – explained using evolutionary concepts via kin selection and reciprocal altruism (an ESS) (see Section 3.1).

Conclusion
- **evolutionary concepts** can explain many behaviours but some behaviours are not affected by natural selection – purely learned behaviours – cultural transmission
- **cultural transmission** is much faster than natural selection – can spread through same generation, e.g. Imo (macaque) washing sweet potatoes (Ridley ('86)).

1.2 Competition for resources

- competition for limited resources is an example of **selection pressure**
- those individuals able to compete effectively for and gain those resources will have increased reproductive output and their genes will increase in the population
- **natural selection acts on competitive ability**.

Exploitation

- where there are sufficient resources, individuals should spread out throughout the resource area – decreased unnecessary competition – resources are exploited more efficiently
- if resources are evenly distributed, the organisms should be too, e.g. wading birds on shore
- if resources are clumped, organisms should be too – but in same proportions as resource
- dispersion of animals reflects the dispersion of the resource = **ideal free distribution**, e.g. Power ('84) catfish feeding on algae, observed in cattle, sheep and bird colonies too
- but – only works up to a point since not all individuals are equal – highest competitive ability likely to be in rich resource areas.

Resource defence

- if scarce resource, effects of competition lessened by **territoriality** and **resource defence**
- **cost – interference** – resource exploitation is interfered with by maintaining territory
- **cost** = energy expenditure in maintaining territory, **benefit** = competitor free resource
- fittest individuals control best territories with most resources
- **optimality model** – resource defence should only occur when benefits outweigh costs, e.g. Gill and Wolf ('75) golden-winged sunbird only defend territory if food scarce
- **optimal territory size** – e.g. hummingbirds adjust territory size depending on weight (increased weight, smaller territory needed).

Aggression

- **competitive ability may be related to aggression** in some species – ability to 'frighten off' competitors
- highest reproductive success if threaten successfully but no actual fight occurs
- **ritualised aggression** reduces likelihood of physical combat, e.g. cat threat displays – exaggerate size, gorillas drumming on chest
  e.g. Clutton-Brock and Albon ('79) red deer ritualised aggression, roaring, parallel walk, combat – either male can retreat at any stage (before injury) – combat only if similar size
- **territoriality** reduces aggression through 'owner wins' strategy
- **dominance hierarchies** reduce aggression – do not challenge unbeatable opponent
- **learning** reduces aggression – lions remember individuals they have lost to before and are not likely to fight them again.

1.3. Predator-prey and symbiotic relationships

a. Predator-prey relationships

- **selection pressure on predator** to catch more prey – fitter and reproduce more
- **selection pressure on prey** to evade predation – survive to reproduce more
- each species evolves according to selection pressure generated by other species characteristics (**coevolution**) – leads to **evolutionary 'arms race'**
- e.g. good prey characteristics, e.g. speed, stamina, camouflage.

Stages of predation

Endler ('91) predator-prey selection pressures at each of 5 stages of predation:

i. **encounter** – coevolution of sensory systems – advantageous for both to detect other from range – sleep may reduce encounter rate (hidden) so evolved in prey (Meddis ('77))

ii. **detection** – camouflage (cryptic colouration) advantageous to both (e.g. leaf frog, chameleon) – predators (e.g. lions) approach prey from downwind (less chance of detection)

Competition can affect distribution of organisms.

When is it worth defending a resource?

When is it worth fighting over a resource?

When 2 species evolve together = coevolution.

iii. **identification** – predator/prey must then be identified as such – some prey species have evolved to mimic unpalatable species, predators to mimic harmless (see below)

iv. **approach** – predator evolves to reach prey as quickly as possible, prey evolve rapid response and groups use confusion strategies (see Section 3.2)

v. **consumption** – predator evolves mechanisms for reaching edible matter (e.g. sea otters use rocks to break open abalone shells) – prey may evolve toxic substances.

Mimicry

Mimics can deter predators or fool their prey.

- **Batesian mimicry** – palatable prey evolves to mimic unpalatable/poisonous species, e.g. hoverfly mimics wasp, hawk moth caterpillar mimics snake
- **Mullerian mimicry** – mildly noxious prey mimics more noxious – universal, honest signal for predator to avoid (e.g. wing patterns in *Heliconius* butterfly species)
- **aggressive mimicry** – predator mimics harmless, e.g. sabre-toothed blenny mimics cleaner wrasse, gets close to large fish and takes bite.

b. Symbiotic relationships

More coevolution.

- interaction of 2 species where both gain (not necessarily same amount) – **mutual benefit**
- natural selection can explain since both benefit
- e.g. cleaner wrasse feeds on ecto-parasites on larger fish (both gain); *Acacia* trees and ants – ants have shelter and food, defend *Acacia* against herbivores
- again, coevolution occurs – some *Acacia* species have evolved nectaries to feed ants
- figs and fig wasps show extreme levels of coevolution – fig species can only be fertilised by particular species of fig wasp, fig wasp can only develop in fig.

Questions

Section 1

1. Explain the mechanism of evolution.

2. What evidence is there to suggest that evolution occurs, and has occurred?

3. Explain how behaviours can evolve.

4. What types of behaviour can be affected by evolution? Give specific examples.

5. How can competition lead to evolution?

6. How do competition and resource distribution interact?

7. When is resource defence likely?

8. Competitive ability may be related to aggression – how have aggressive behaviours evolved to reduce harm?

9. Explain the evolutionary 'arms race' in a predator-prey relationship.

10. What are the 5 stages of predation that selection can act on.

11. Explain the 3 types of mimicry, and how they evolved.

12. What is a symbiotic relationship?

13. Give examples of coevolution in symbiotic relationships.

Test yourself – then check your answers.

2 | Reproductive strategies

2.1 Sexual selection in evolution

- individuals that have characteristics making them more likely to reproduce are more likely to pass their genes on to the next generation = **sexual selection**
- the specific desirable characteristics depend on a number of factors, e.g. sex, mating strategy
- **intra-sexual selection** = selection occurring within a sex – mate competition
- **inter-sexual selection** = mate choice drives selection.

Intra-sexual strategies = mate competition
- mate competition is likely for the sex that can potentially have a great number of successful reproductive encounters – usually males compete for access to females
- male mate competition often occurs in polygynous systems (see Section 2.3).

Results of intra-sexual selection
- **aggression** – prior to mating, males compete, bigger/stronger males are more likely to win and gain access to females – can lead to **evolution of weapons** or **sexual dimorphism**
  e.g. red deer – large antlers evolved, used in mate competition, 1½ times female size
- **sperm competition** – after mating, if the female has been inseminated by more than one male, their sperm will compete to fertilise the egg(s)
- e.g. parasitic worm species uses copulatory plug – seals female after copulation
- e.g. some damselfly species remove competitor's sperm using appendage on penis.

> Male competition has resulted in a variety of adaptations evolving.

Inter-sexual selection = mate choice
- females usually choose mates – usually have **lower reproductive potential, higher investment per offspring** – leads to selection for ability to choose suitable mate
- choices made by females determine which males pass on genes to next generation – **selection pressure on males** for features chosen by females
- features may be useful (e.g. size) or not (e.g. peacock's tail).

> The "choosy" sex drives the evolution of the opposite sex.

a. Fisher's hypothesis ('30) – 'good taste', 'sexy sons'
- to explain bizarre features, e.g. elaborate tails etc. of many male birds – **tails reduce survival, but increase reproductive success** so runaway process occurs
- females mating with attractive (but hindered) male will produce sons that mate successfully (if mate with non-hindered male produce sons that will not mate)
- e.g. Andersson ('82) manipulated tails of long-tailed widow birds, longer tails, more mating.

b. Handicap hypothesis – 'good genes', 'good sense'
- Zahavi ('75) females prefer males with handicap – in order to survive with handicap must be very fit – i.e. **handicap reliable measure of survival ability**
- Hamilton and Zuk ('82) sexual displays reliably indicate genetic **resistance to disease**.

c. Symmetry – 'good genes'
- Moller ('92) sexual displays are good indicators of symmetry – **symmetry is a good indicator of 'good genes' and development**
- e.g. symmetrical human faces more attractive.

Human sexual selection
- **female** reproductive capacity is affected by age, physical features used by males to judge age and therefore reproductive potential
- **male** reproductive capacity not affected by age, females should choose males who can provide resources for offspring
- Dunbar ('95) evidence for males offering resources and seeking attractiveness, females vice versa – lonely hearts adverts.

2.2 Parental investment in the rearing of the young

Trivers ('72) **parental investment = effort put into rearing individual offspring
parental effort = total parental effort during lifetime**
Females tend to have high parental effort, males high mating effort.
reproductive effort = mating effort + parental effort.

Investment in gametes is unequal = anisogamy
- female gametes (eggs) are usually larger and cost more to produce than male gametes (sperm), e.g. ostrich egg is several cm diameter, sperm is microscopic
- females more likely to care for fertilised eggs – males can easily mate again, not much investment lost, females may not mate again this season or lose larger investment.

Mating strategy affects parental investment
- Krebs and Davies ('93) summarise generalised effects: **monogamy = both parents** (birds), **polygyny = female only** (mammals), **polygamy/promiscuity = male only** (fish)
- **birds** – reproductive success determined by food supply to young – both provide food, reproductive output doubles, e.g. kittiwake pairs for life (Coulson ('66))
- **mammals** – viviparous with period of gestation in female, further female investment in lactation – males often desert and polygyny occurs
- **fish** – usually no parental care, either sex may provide a little – female if internal fertilisation, male if external.

Fertilisation systems affect parental investment (Gross and Shine ('81))
- **paternity certainty hypothesis** – male should only provide parental care if certain of paternity – may be more certain with external fertilisation (sperm competition effects internal)
- **order of gamete release hypothesis** – Dawkins and Carlisle ('76) males desert with internal fertilisation, but sperm must be released after eggs for external fertilisation to occur – female has chance to desert first
- **association hypothesis** – Williams ('75) internal fertilisation, female preadapted – external fertilisation, male often territorial, preadapted to guard eggs.

ESS model of parental investment
- Maynard-Smith ('77) developed an ESS model of parental investment – **investment of one parent depends on strategy of other**, on **number of offspring** and on **probability of survival of offspring** on staying or leaving
- there are several alternative ESSs, depending on these factors
- e.g. both should desert if the female can lay more eggs if she deserts and the male is likely to have more offspring surviving (total) by finding another mate.

2.3 Mating strategies and social organisation

Mating systems
a. **monogamy** – pair bond between single male and single female, e.g. swans
b. **polygamy** – single member of one sex pairs with several of opposite sex
   i. **polygyny** – single male, several females – most common polygamy
     simultaneous polygyny = harem, e.g. elephant seal, **serial polygyny** = several, separate females mated with over season, e.g. pied flycatcher
   ii. **polyandry** – single female, several males – rare – e.g. lily trotting jacana
c. **promiscuity** – males and females mate with several members of opposite sex – males gain by impregnating many females, females gain due to sperm competition, e.g. dunnock
d. **polygynandry** – as for promiscuity, but living in social groups with long-term bonds, e.g. chimpanzee
- **problem** – not all members of species use same strategy, so cannot classify whole

Females usually invest more in offspring.

species as using one system, e.g. Davies and Lunberg ('84) all 4 strategies in dunnocks
- **problem** – definition is one-sided, e.g. serial polygyny for male, female = monogamous
- better to define **mating strategies** – individuals use strategy suited to particular situation.

Mating strategies

- best strategy depends on a number of factors – **food availability and distribution**, **parental investment**, **sexual selection**
- strategies include those listed above, but others exist too
- **sneak copulation** – if large males fight to gain access to females, small males will never win – only gain access to females by sneak strategy, e.g. elephant seals, digger wasps
- **dimorphic form** – sneak strategy evolved further – e.g. Coho salmon, 2 male forms: large, fighting form and small, sneaking form – both forms fertilise eggs – ESS
- **sex change** – some species alter sex during lifetime – e.g. Fricke ('79) protandrous hermaphroditism in anemonefish
- **environment** – three-spined stickleback brighter red preferred by females but more predation – bright red found in dull light (deep water) conditions, dull red in bright light.

Mating strategies and social organisation

- **food availability** – Crook ('64) weaver birds – scarce, dispersed food = solitary feeding and monogamy, clumped food = group living, competition and polygyny
- Jarman ('74) similar results with ungulates
- **simultaneous polygyny – harems** of one male and several females, stronger males have bigger harems – competition fierce for control of harems, often control does not last long
- harems may be permanent, e.g. Dunbar ('84) baboons, or seasonal, e.g. red deer
- harem has **dominance hierarchy** – dominant male = harem master, dominant female has most offspring
- **polygyny – lek** = very small territory (aggregated) used for display to females – females choose mate (gain good genes) – few males mate repeatedly, some not at all
- **polyandry** – spotted sandpiper females mate with several males, leave eggs with males – females compete for males
- **dispersal – polygynous species** – young males disperse to find new group of females
- **territories may be inherited** by male offspring – if so, females disperse.

2.4 Parent-offspring conflict

- **parents' best interests** to ensure survival of all offspring (including future offspring) but **offspring's best interests** to maximise own survival see Section 4.4
- **offspring behaviour** evolves to gain maximum benefits from parents
- **parenting behaviour** evolves to maximise number of offspring surviving.

Pre-natal conflict

- human foetuses can cause pre-eclampsia and gestational diabetes (see Section 4.4).

Weaning conflict

- **offspring gain** if fed for longer, **parents gain** if stop feeding as soon as offspring can feed itself – maximises future reproductive potential
- langur baboon infants **shriek** and slap mother to gain food, human infant **crying and tantrums**
- **deceit** – herring gull chicks crouch (look smaller) to encourage parents to feed them
- **age of parent affects conflict** – older mothers have lower future reproductive output, invest more in present offspring

Optimum mating strategy varies.

Parent-offspring conflict can be explained in evolutionary terms.

- Alexander ('74) **parental behaviour drives system** – those who succumb to infant produce fewer offspring, genes do not increase frequency.

Sibling conflict
- **siblings compete for parental investment** – more siblings, less investment per individual
- an individual removing its siblings would gain more food and increase survival
- Mock and Parker ('86) siblicide in egrets – advantageous if a sibling remains – if only one left in nest, parents abandon and start again.

Infanticide
- **observed in harems**, e.g. male lion takes over harem, kills cubs from previous male – does not waste investment on another's genes – also, females ovulate sooner
- **obvious benefit to male**, not to female – decreases reproductive output
- **pseudo-oestrus** shown by some pregnant lionesses, new male does not commit infanticide – paternity uncertain
- **Bruce effect** ('60) pregnant mice reabsorb developing embryos if encounter new male urine – may be good predictor of infanticide so lose less investment by reabsorbing
- raptors often feed largest chicks (first eggs) most – smaller may starve and be fed to older siblings.

Examples of infanticide.

Questions

Test yourself – then check your answers.

Section 2

1. Explain sexual selection.

2. What are the consequences of intra-sexual selection (mate competition)?

3. What are the explanations for evolution of features by inter-sexual selection (mate choice)?

4. What evidence is there to suggest that sexual selection is a force in human evolution?

5. How does anisogamy affect parental investment?

6. How does mating strategy affect parental investment?

7. How can the system of fertilisation affect parental investment?

8. Describe the ESS model of parental investment.

9. List the types of mating system.

10. What additional mating strategies exist?

11. How is mating strategy linked with social organisation?

12. Why does parent-offspring conflict arise?

13. What are the main areas of parent-offspring conflict?

14. Explain weaning conflict in evolutionary terms (use examples).

15. Explain infanticide in evolutionary terms (use examples).

3 | Kinship and social behaviour

3.1 Apparent altruism

Altruism = increasing chance of survival of another while decreasing own.
Paradox of altruism – natural selection predicts animals behave selfishly, but altruism occurs. Several explanations for altruistic behaviour.

Group selection
* (Wynne-Edwards '62) altruism increases survival of group – now disregarded since natural selection operates at the level of the individual.

Kin selection
* Hamilton ('63) if increase **survival of kin**, increase spread of (some of) own genes
* Dawkins ('76) **selfish gene** – altruism towards kin benefits genes of individuals but not individuals themselves – increases inclusive fitness (fitness of gene pool)
* altruism is not altruistic at level of gene – '**apparent altruism**'
* **recognition of kin** required – Stuart ('91) spatial proximity and phenotype matching; Holmes and Sherman ('82) association mechanism.

Reciprocal altruism
* Trivers ('71) A helps B at a cost to self, expectation of return at later date
* Wilkinson ('84) vampire bats regurgitate food for one another (cost to individual) – if all do this, all benefit – but why don't cheats evolve and spread throughout population?
* Axelrod and Hamilton ('81) **Prisoner's Dilemma** used to investigate evolutionarily stable strategies (ESS) – defector using alternative strategy cannot gain advantage and spread
* **tit-for-tat** is an ESS – individual behaves how opponent did on last meeting.

Mutualism
* **both individuals gain** from interaction – **not true altruism**
* can be same species, e.g. 2 pied wagtails defend large feeding territory (gain food)
* co-operation can decrease predation, e.g. geese grazing, mobbing behaviour (Section 3.2)
* can be inter-species, e.g. cleaner fish picks parasites of larger predator (both gain).

Induced altruism (manipulated altruism)
* **unintentional** on part of altruist – **not true altruism**
* **brood parasitism** – Brooke and Davies ('91) dunnock raising cuckoo chick
* **parasitism** – human provides food and shelter for tapeworm
* **mimics** – Holldobler ('71) beetle grub mimics begging ant, gains food from worker.

3.2 Sociality in non-human animals

Social co-operation in hunting and foraging
* groups can **locate and capture** food more easily
* an individual spends **less time** being vigilant in a group – **more time** feeding, e.g. house sparrows (Elgar, '86)
* **information centre** – Ward and Zahavi ('73) communal birds gain info. about feeding sites
* lionesses in groups have **increased capture rate** and **increase in size of prey** (Section 3.1)
* **cost** (sharing) and **benefit** (more food) – see optimality models below.

Social co-operation in defence against predators
* **increased vigilance** – Bertram ('80) ostriches – overall vigilance increases with group

size, but each individual spends less time being vigilant
- **groups spot predators earlier**, e.g. pigeons spotting goshawks
- **dilution – safety in numbers** – probability of individual being taken by predator decreases as group increases
- Neill and Cullen ('74) middle of group safer than edge
- **group defence**, e.g. buffalo face outwards and form defensive ring around young
- **mobbing behaviour**, e.g. black-headed gulls attack crows near their nests (Kruuk ('64)).

Optimality model (see Section 4.2)
- as group size alters the **costs and benefits alter**
- increased group size results in: increased benefit of **sharing vigilance**; increased cost of **conspicuousness**; decreased benefit from **sharing food**; increased benefit from **defence**
- **optimality model** used to predict strategies in different situations
- **optimum group size** varies depending on the situation.

Group living has costs and benefits.

3.3 Imprinting and bonding

Imprinting
- **form of learning by which young precocial animals form attachments to parent**
- **innate tendency**, e.g. chicks follow first moving object seen, after following for 10 minutes have formed a permanent attachment, have imprinted on object
- Lorenz ('35) suggested a **critical period** – imprinting must occur within a given time period (varies from species to species) and easy, rapid learning during this time
- **sensitive period** more flexible than critical period – time when learning more easily occurs – Sluckin and Salzen ('61) showed critical period could be extended if chicks raised in isolation
- following parent should lead to increased survival – keeps out of danger, learns appropriate behaviours = **filial imprinting**
- **sexual imprinting** – identifies which species to mate with, Immelman ('72) cross-fostered finches preferred to mate with foster species
- but turkeys imprinted on humans readily mate with other turkeys
- Sluckin and Salzen ('61) irreversible form of learning, but Guiton ('66) showed imprinting can be reversed
- Hess ('68) **law of effort** – more effort in following results in a stronger bond.

Rapid, inflexible learning.

Bonding
- **attachment bonds** take longer to form (can be months) than imprinting bonds (minutes)
- attachment bonds occur in altricial species (cannot move independently when newborn)
- an emotional bond is formed
- there is a sensitive period for bond formation
- physical contact is important for the development of a bond – Harlow ('59) rhesus monkeys
- comfort is more important than food-giving – Harlow ('59) wire and cloth mothers
- **failure to bond** can result in inappropriate behaviour patterns – Harlow ('59) mating difficulties and poor parenting in deprived (un-bonded) rhesus monkeys
- attachment bonds are important for human infants also (Bowlby, '69) – see Chapter 6, Section 1.1.

Emotional bond too.

3.4 Signalling systems in non-human animals

- **a signal transmits information** from one individual to another (not always intentional) and alters the probability of a behaviour occurring in the receiver

- many different types of signalling system: visual, auditory, olfactory, tactile, electrical
- different signalling systems have evolved in different environments.

Evolution of signals
- signals are derived from other behaviours:
  - **i. intention movements** – first step of behaviour becomes ritualised signal for that behaviour
  - **ii. antithesis** – opposite behaviour has opposite meaning, e.g. threat/submission displays
  - **iii. displacement activities** – conflicting behaviours result in another behaviour
  - **iv. autonomic displays** – unconscious, but signal emotional state, e.g. effects of adrenalin
- **ritualisation** – signal is stereotypical and predicts future behaviour – lacks ambiguity
- signalling must be evolutionarily advantageous (increase survival) in order to evolve
- **courtship signals** prevent waste of resources mating with other species
- **threat displays** prevent actual fights and actual harm – increase survival rate
- **alarm calls** increase individual fitness in groups (see Sections 3.1 and 3.2).

Honesty
- **honest signals** will evolve into ritualised, unambiguous behaviours
- increased correct interpretation, increased survival, increase in gene pool
- dishonest signals not dominant since not an ESS (see Section 3.1)
- Dawkins and Krebs ('78) **manipulation hypothesis** – signals given to manipulate behaviour of receiver to maximise benefit to signaller, if more than threshold % dishonest signal, signal ignored
- other examples of dishonest signals: prey may stand tall in front of predator (seem larger), partridge fakes broken wing and lures fox away from nest.

Efficiency of signalling mechanisms

Method	Range	Speed	Flow over barrier?	Used at night?
visual	med	v. fast	N	N (unusual)
auditory	long	fast	Y	Y
olfactory	long	slow	Y	Y
tactile	short	v. fast	N	Y

Information available from signalling systems

Method	Fade out	Locatability	Cost	Exploitability
visual	fast	easy	low–med	high
auditory	fast	fairly easy	high	med
olfactory	slow	difficult	low	low
tactile	fast	easy	low	low

Auditory is best method but has high cost, olfactory methods last longest so useful for territoriality.

Visual signals
- **good lighting conditions** required so not found in nocturnal or deep sea animals for example
- **threat and submission displays** seen in, e.g. dogs, Siamese fighting fish
- **identification** – markings may identify species or individuals
- **reproductive state** – e.g. female baboons have swollen genitalia during oestrus
- **courtship displays** – beak wiping in Galapagos finches, peacock tails
- **alarm** – white tails exposed in rabbits and antelopes

Communication of information increases survival.

Receptor, signal and signaller must all evolve together.

Some signals can be exploited by predators.

- **warning colouration** – indicates distasteful/dangerous, e.g. yellow and black of wasp
- **food location** – waggle dance of honey bees (see Section 4.3)
- **feeding** – herring gull beak elicits pecking in young, leads to regurgitation of food
- **emotion** – blushing in humans, octopus colouration changes with mood.

Auditory signals
- **alarm calls** (see Section 4.3) – e.g. many bird species, vervet monkeys, whales
- **aggression** – hissing in cats, growling in dogs
- **group cohesion** – humpback whale group sings same song which evolves over time
- **territoriality** – e.g. male blackbirds sing, red deer stags roar
- **mate location** – male birdsong also attracts females, some whales use songs to locate mates
- **specific messages** – human language, messages in chimpanzees (Marler ('76) identified 13)
- **echolocation** – used to find food by bats.

Olfactory signals
- **territoriality** – urination in dogs
- **mate location** – pheromones in moths
- **reproductive state** – female baboons release chemicals during oestrus
- **identification** – bees recognise members of hive
- **food location** – ants leave pheromone trails from food, can be followed by others.

Tactile signals
- **group cohesion** – maintenance of dominance hierarchies in primates
- **location** – gerbils use vibrissae to explore
- **courtship** – beak tapping in albatross, stickleback females only lay eggs if prodded by male
- **bonding** – contact required for bonding, also reduction of anxiety.

Electrical signals
- **food location** – e.g. by duck-billed platypus.

Section 3

1. What is the paradox of altruism?

2. What are the explanations for altruistic behaviour?

3. Explain how kin selection accounts for altruistic behaviour.

4. Explain the evolution of reciprocal altruism.

5. What are the advantages and disadvantages of social cooperation in hunting/foraging?

6. What are the advantages and disadvantages of social cooperation in defence against predators?

7. How does optimality assess costs/benefits in terms of group size?

8. Describe the two types of imprinting.

9. What are the main features of imprinting?

10. What are the important features of bonding?

11. Why have signalling systems evolved?

12. Signals have evolved for use in a number of situations – list them.

13. What is the importance of honesty in signalling?

14. Give examples of the use of visual signals.

15. Give examples of the use of auditory signals.

4 | Behaviour analysis

S – R links.

4.1 Classical and operant conditioning – Learning Theory

a. Classical conditioning
- form of learning based on **stimulus-response associations**
- initially, UCS (unconditioned stimulus) produces UCR (unconditioned response)
- CS (conditioned stimulus) repeatedly paired with UCS
- CS produces CR (conditioned response) – CS now associated with CR
- important features: **generalisation**; **discrimination**; **extinction**; **spontaneous recovery**
- does not require conscious thought – often autonomic responses involved
- **forward conditioning** – CS just before and during UCS (strongest learning)
- **backward conditioning** – CS just after UCS (little learning)
- **simultaneous conditioning** – CS and UCS at same time (some learning)
- **trace conditioning** – CS first, but stopped before UCS (little learning)
- **one trial-learning** – special case – single exposure leads to strong association – particularly powerful or traumatic event required (e.g. vomiting).

For
- Pavlov's experiments ('27) – dogs, saliva, bell etc.
- Menzies ('37) vaso-constriction in humans
- Watson and Raynor ('20) Little Albert and rat
- uses in behaviour therapy – systematic desensitisation, aversion and implosion therapy

Against
- expectation and predictability are important – implies cognitive factors (Rescorla ('68) learning only if tone predicts shock)
- preparedness – more prepared to learn certain associations (Seligman ('70))
- Shapiro et al. ('80) pigeon preparedness

b. Operant conditioning
- **trial and error learning**
- sequence of events: 1. **antecedents** 2. **operant** 3. **consequences**
- all reinforcement increases likelihood of behaviour occurring again
- punishment decreases likelihood of behaviour occurring again
- **positive reinforcement = reward** (pleasant stimulus)
- **negative reinforcement** – two types:
  escape = removal of unpleasant stimulus
  avoidance = avoidance of unpleasant, using predictor/cue
- **punishment** – suppresses behaviour, does not remove, cannot learn new behaviours
- **schedules of reinforcement** – variable more resistant to extinction
- **shaping** – successive approximations towards desired behaviour
- **extinction**, **generalisation** and **discrimination** as for classical conditioning.

Secondary reinforcers can drive operant conditioning through association with primary reinforcers.

For
- Skinner ('38) operant chamber experiments with rats, pigeons, levers etc. – showed most of points above
- Miller ('48) avoidance learning in rats

Against
- Seligman ('75) cognitive factors can be involved – learned helplessness
- preparedness as for classical

Problems with Learning Theory as a whole (i.e. Classical and Operant)
- cannot explain **insight learning** – problem solving rather than trial and error or S–R links
- cannot explain **latent learning** – learning without reward – Tolman ('32) cognitive maps
- cannot explain **imitation** or observational learning – social learning theory.

4.2 Learning in the natural environment (foraging and homing)

Behaviour in the natural environment can be innate or learned. Learning does occur in the natural environment – when behaviours are modified by experience. Examples of behaviours which can be modified are foraging and homing. Modification of behaviours is due to learning – there are many types:

- **classical conditioning** (Section 4.1)
- **operant conditioning** (Section 4.1)
- **imprinting** (Section 3.3)
- **habituation** – learning not to respond
- **insight learning** (Section 4.1 – problems with Learning Theory).

a. Foraging behaviour

- **foraging = finding and collecting food**
- **handling time** – limits amount of food collected per unit time
- **profitabilit**y of prey = net energy value divided by handling time
- **search image** – learned – used for distinguishing food from background rapidly
- **innate recognition** shown by some, e.g. toads and small, moving objects (usually insects)
- **searching behaviour** – innate or learned – various strategies: Smith ('74) thrush moves forward with dispersed food, turns when eating clumped food (likely to find more)
- **optimum foraging strategy** – should be able to predict animal's behaviour with information on body and mouth size, food size, handling time, food density and spacing etc
- OFS applies to many foraging behaviours – e.g. Zach ('79) crows and whelks, dropping height
- OFS provides testable predictions and can often generalise to other species.

> Optimum foraging strategy depends on a number of factors.

b. Homing behaviour

- used to return to home (nest, burrow etc.) – implies **memory** of home and **navigation**
- advantage = return to safe, known area (less likely to be killed), large scale migration for increased food or safer breeding area
- can be exhibited daily, monthly, annually – shown over few metres or 1000s of miles
- various **cues** are used for navigation (list below)
  memorised landmarks – Tinbergen and Kruyt ('38) digger wasps and pine cones
  sun –Gwinner and Wiltschko ('80) caged warblers' migratory restlessness – correct orientation
  stars – lesser whitethroat in planetarium, star map affects flight path
  magnetism – pigeons disoriented if small magnet on head
  mineral detection – Hasler ('60) salmon returning to rivers – less accurate if nose plugged
  ultrasound – birds can use long-distance sounds to navigate
- **hierarchy of cues** – e.g. sun, but magnetism if cloudy – sun, but stars if night
- homing pigeons provide much research into true navigation
- Perdeck ('67) juvenile starlings show innate directional orientation but adults show true navigation – requires learning and memory.

> A variety of mechanisms have been shown to aid homing accuracy.

4.3 Animal language

Definition of language

Not simply communication – many animals communicate – not just signalling. Argued that it is species specific to humans. Others argue other higher primates also possess cognitive abilities required for language.

Hockett ('59) several design features of language:

vocal/auditory	broadcast/directional
rapid fading	total feedback
interchangeability (give and receive)	specialisation (not a by-product)
semanticity	arbitrariness
traditional transmission	learnability
discreteness (separate units built up)	duality of patterning (organisation levels)
displacement (refer to items not here)	productivity (can create novel)
prevarication (can create lies)	reflexiveness (can describe self).

Displacement rules out most animal communication – usually refer to present situation, e.g. courtship rituals, threat/submission displays, alarm calls.

Studies of natural animal language

Honeybee
- language system (dance) informs others of food location (von Frisch ('67), Gould ('76))
- **round dance** – food within 50m, not specific location, others find by olfaction
- **waggle dance** – precise location, figure of eight, angle of central axis to vertical = path to food compared to sun position, number of waggles indicates distance
- does not show all of Hockett's features – e.g. not vocal, reflexive, do not lie.

Alarm calls
- some alarm calls are **general** – similar calls by many species of bird, many recognise
- some alarm calls are **specific** – different for different predators, produce different responses
- Struhsaker ('67) vervet monkeys have unambiguous calls for predators, e.g. snake, leopard
- Seyfarth et al. ('80) vervet responses to calls are appropriate – look up after 'eagle' call.

Birdsong
- birdsong has many functions including territory marking, alarm calls and begging for food
- most birdsong has an **innate component** which is **refined through imitation** (Slater ('81))
- birdsong does not show many of Hockett's features.

Attempts to teach human language to non-human animals
- most attempts have involved higher primates. A few studies into other animal groups have been performed, with little success – e.g. Lilly ('65) trained dolphin, Pepperberg ('53) trained African grey parrot
- Gardner and Gardner ('69) Washoe (chimpanzee) learned American Sign Language (ASL) – 130 signs by five years by imitation and reinforcement – combined words to make phrases, did not consistently apply grammar, did refer to items not present (displacement), argument over novel utterances (productivity)
- Premack and Premack ('72) Sarah (chimpanzee) – shapes on board – produced 2-3 word sentences, answered questions, problem with word order, did not initiate conversations

- Rumbaugh et al. ('73) Lana taught with lexigrams (patterns representing words) – could differentiate word order – does this imply understanding or simple operant conditioning?
- Patterson ('79) Koko (gorilla) 7 years old used 700 ASL signs, passed on signing to another gorilla, Michael (transmission), both signed to one another, would start conversations, Koko lied, used swear words and invented 20 new words
- Savage-Rumbaugh ('91) Kanzi (bonobo) learned lexigrams – 11 years old knows 200 words, responds to complex requests, some understanding of word order, ability of young child (remember brain only third size of human)
- Terrace et al. ('79) provide another view – Nim Chimpsky taught ASL – argued simply operant conditioning, as is all research – non-humans do not possess LAD.

4.4 Evolutionary explanations of human behaviour

- an attempt to explain human behaviour in terms of its **adaptive significance**
- observed behaviours have evolved and therefore have a genetic component – this may be a predisposition to perform a behaviour rather than total pre-programming
- many behaviours have been explained in this way, e.g. altruism, mating strategies, prejudice, attachment, parenting behaviour, sleep, language, host–parasite relationships.

Altruism – in humans can be explained by **kin-selection**, **reciprocal altruism**, **mutualism** (see Section 3.1 – non-human altruism)

Mating strategies – different mating strategies evolved in different situations:
- **very harsh conditions – polyandry** in Tibet (woman marries brothers) – 2 men needed to manage farm (Dickemann ('85)) – rare strategy
- **society with powerful men – polygyny** (harem) – powerful men mate with many females, females gain since offspring gain wealth and fitness (**kin selection**)
- **hunter-gatherer** – limited resources (male cannot support more than 1 female) – **monogamy**
- humans show some **sexual dimorphism** (size diff. between sexes) indicates some **polygyny**.

Sexual selection – mate choice
- female should evolve to choose male providing most resources (fittest offspring – kin-selection), male evolve to choose young female (most fertile)
- physical attractiveness may be used to assess fitness of mate.

Prejudice – can be explained by kin-selection (see Section 3.1) – increased inclusive fitness.

Parent–offspring conflict
- **mother** evolved to produce as many offspring as possible – most genes in next generation – limit investment in this child so can have more – **ensure future reproductive potential**
- **offspring** evolved to gain as much parental investment as possible – **maximise own fitness** (and fitness of own genes), while not killing parent
- **pre-natal conflict** – foetus may cause mother to crave/avoid certain foods to satisfy needs, may cause pre-eclampsia (high blood pressure) so more blood to placenta, also gestational diabetes (high sugar levels – for use by foetus – increased survival)
- **conflict in childhood** – parent should invest in all offspring, child has increased survival if more parental investment – crying to gain attention and resources – smiling for same
- **age of child** affects investment – much at first since dies otherwise (waste of resources).

Different conditions result in different mating strategies.

Parents – offspring relationships are not 100% harmonious!

Attachment (see Section 3.3, Chapter 6, Section 1.1) – increase **survival**, **gain attention** and **learn appropriate behaviours** – learn to **avoid siblings in sexual relationships** (sibling mating – increase genetic disorders, reduce fitness), evolved to avoid.

Problem with explanation

- learning is a major factor for human behaviour – evolutionary approach mainly ignores effects of experience
- but – can have a genetic predisposition to learn – innate component making certain behaviours more easily learned (preparedness) – e.g. innate component of intelligence.

Evolution cannot explain all human behaviour.

Questions

Test yourself – then check your answers.

Section 4

1. What are the main components of classical conditioning?

2. Explain 2 problems for classical conditioning.

3. What are the main components of operant conditioning?

4. Give evidence for operant conditioning.

5. What are the general problems of learning theory?

6. What are the important aspects of foraging behaviour?

7. What are the important aspects of homing behaviour?

8. List Hockett's design features of language.

9. Give examples of natural animal language and assess it in terms of Hockett's features.

10. Give positive and negative arguments on the view that non-human animals can be taught language.

11. Which human behaviours have been explained in evolutionary terms?

12. Explain the evolution of the parent-offspring conflict.

13. What are the problems with an evolutionary explanation of human behaviour?

Chapter three

Bio-psychology

1 | Basic neural and hormonal processes and their influence on behaviour

1.1 CNS, ANS and endocrine system

Central nervous system (CNS)
- **CNS = brain and spinal cord**, consists of 10-12 billion nerve cells (neurones)
- 80% of neurones in brain, particularly cortex
- CNS connected to rest of body via peripheral nervous system (PNS): autonomic and somatic
- brain can be subdivided into 3 different regions (forebrain, midbrain, hindbrain):

1. forebrain
  i. **cerebral hemispheres** (joined by corpus callosum)
     cortex responsible for **higher functions** – thought, memory, problem solving, language
     cortex is subdivided into four lobes: frontal; parietal; occipital; temporal
     contralateral control in somatosensory and motor cortices (L brain associated with R body)
  ii. **thalamus** – links cerebral hemispheres and sense organs, sleep/wake function
  iii. **hypothalamus** – important for homeostasis and motivation, links CNS and ANS, endocrine function
  iv. **limbic system** – group of structures (inc. hypoth. and thal.), involved in need satisfaction (feeding, mating, escaping), similar to primitive mammal brains, olfactory region.

2. midbrain
- reticular activating system (RAS) important for sleep/wake, habituation, attention.

3. hindbrain
- **cerebellum** – coordination and fine control of motor activity, balance
- **pons varioli** – connects 2 hemispheres of cerebellum
- **medulla oblongata** – extension of spinal cord, control of autonomic functions.

Autonomic nervous system (ANS)
- **links CNS and internal environment of body**
- important for homeostasis and autonomic (automatic) functions
- two branches: sympathetic and parasympathetic nervous systems
- **sympathetic branch** prepares body for action – fight or flight – e.g. heart rate up
- **parasympathetic branch** prepares for rest – e.g. heart rate down, increased digestion.

Endocrine (hormone) system
- **hormones = chemicals** – affect regions of body in different ways, affect behaviour
- hormones secreted into bloodstream by **endocrine glands**:
  i. **pituitary gland** – 'master' gland – hormones produced control release of hormones from other glands, e.g. ACTH affects adrenal glands, also releases direct acting hormones, e.g. ADH, growth hormone
  ii. **pineal gland** – serotonin and melatonin – activity cycles
  iii. **pancreas** – insulin and glucagon – controls blood glucose levels
  iv. **adrenal glands** – cortex secretes steroids – stress response and salt balance, medulla secretes adrenalin and noradrenalin – sympathetic NS neurotransmitters.

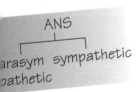

1.2 Influences on physiological and behavioural functions

The CNS, ANS and endocrine systems interact and affect behaviour in many ways.

Physiological effects
- **homeostasis (maintenance of a constant internal environment)**
- several homeostatic mechanisms, e.g. water, salt, sugar, temperature regulation
- homeostasis can involve hypothalamus (CNS), ANS and endocrine system
- e.g. glucose level in blood increases, detected by pancreas cells – secrete insulin, liver converts glucose to glycogen (storage), glucose level drops
- e.g. high concentration of blood detected by osmoreceptors in hypothalamus (CNS), pituitary secretes ADH (endocrine), kidney reabsorbs more water, blood conc. decreases
- fight or flight – detection of danger (CNS), secretion of adrenalin by adrenal glands (endocrine), several physiological effects, e.g. increases heart rate and blood, blood diverted to brain and muscles, from skin and gut pressure – all via ANS.

Behavioural effects
- **homeostatic mechanisms can affect behaviour** – e.g. only so much water can be reabsorbed – eventually drinking is necessary to maintain correct balance – linked to motivation
- hypothalamus detects high blood concentration – behavioural effect = drinking
- feeding regulatory centre in ventro-medial hypothalamus affects eating behaviour, due to glucose/fat levels in blood (damage to area linked to overeating = hyperphagia)
- stomach distension can reduce eating behaviour (not so in obese (Schachter ('68)).
- temperature regulation – detection by preoptic area – behaviour affected, e.g. add/remove clothes, move to shade/sun (or fire)
- sleep/wake behaviour affected by CNS (see Section 3.3)
- menstrual cycle – argument over whether or not this affects behaviour.

1.3 Neuronal and synaptic activity

Neurones

Information is transmitted via neurones and synapses.

- **neurones = nerve cells** – cell body and projections to connect to other cells (up to metre long)
- conduct electrical impulses
- **axon** of neurone ends in **synaptic knobs** – transmit info. to neighbouring neurone
- **sensory neurone** – conducts impulse from receptor (sensory cell) to CNS
- **intermediate neurone** – CNS consists of mainly these, no long projections, many short ones
- **motor neurone** – conducts impulse from CNS to effector (muscle or gland)
- **nerve = bundle of nerve fibres**.

Nerve impulse
- neurones 'at rest' actively expel sodium ions in exchange for potassium ions via sodium/potassium pump, some potassium diffuses back in
- generates imbalance of charge across membrane (in = –ve) = **resting potential** = 70mV
- if neurone stimulated, pump switches off and sodium channels open – sodium ions rush in
- membrane polarity is reversed (now –ve outside cell) = **action potential**
- action potential travels along axon to synaptic knob – only travel in one direction,
- pump switches back on again, restores resting potential.

Synapse
- **synapse = communication between two neurones**
- impulse arrives at synaptic knob, neurotransmitter released into synaptic cleft
- neurotransmitter diffuses across to post-synaptic membrane, attaches to receptor sites

- if excitatory synapse, depolarises post-synaptic membrane, generates action potential
- threshold level of depolarisation needed to generate action potential
  spatial summation – neurotransmitter released from more than 1 synapse – add together to reach threshold; **temporal summation** – synapses add together if in close enough succession
- **all-or-nothing law** – action potential is fired off or not, always the same size and speed
- **stimulus intensity** signalled by frequency of action potentials.

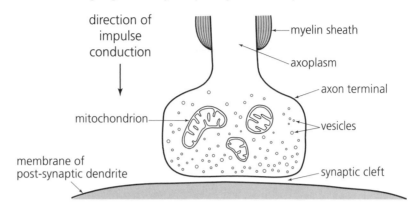

Figure 3.1 Diagram of a synapse

Neurotransmitters

- many different chemicals act as neurotransmitters (>30)
- bind to specific receptor sites on post-synaptic membrane
- rapidly removed and recycled by pre-synaptic knob
- some neurotransmitters are **excitatory**, e.g. acetylcholine in parasympathetic n.s.
- some are **inhibitory**, e.g. dopamine, noradrenalin, endorphins.

1.4 Effects of drugs on behaviour

- **psychoactive drugs = drugs that affect behaviour via brain**
- many different types of psychoactive drugs, affect behaviour in many different ways

> *Effects of drugs depend on individual.*

> *Different drugs affect neuronal activity in different ways.*

- some **imitate excitatory neurotransmitters**, e.g. nicotine imitates adrenalin, stimulates post-synaptic membrane, increases heart rate
- some **stimulate release of neurotransmitter**, increasing excitation of post-synaptic membrane, e.g. amphetamine stimulates noradrenalin release and feeling of euphoria
- some **block neurotransmitters' receptor sites**, preventing them from stimulating post-synaptic membrane, e.g. curare blocks acetylcholine, prevents muscle contraction
- some **prevent reuptake of neurotransmitter** by pre-synaptic knob – continued stimulation of post-synaptic, e.g. cocaine prevents noradrenalin and dopamine reuptake
- some **prevent neurotransmitter breakdown** by enzymes – continued stimulation of post-synaptic, e.g. nerve gas prevents breakdown of acetylcholine.

Psychoactive drugs can also be classified according to the type of effect they have – some have clinical uses, others are abused (outside socially acceptable limits).

Classes listed by Julien (1992)

> *Classification by effect.*

- **anti-depressants**, e.g. monoamine oxidase inhibitors tricyclics serotonin reuptake inhibitors – all increase serotonin levels – increase arousal
- **CNS depressants**, e.g. barbiturates (RAS and neural thresholds depressed – decreases arousal), alcohol (depresses inhibitory synapses – elation)
- **anti-anxiety**, e.g. benzodiazepines (e.g. diazepam = Valium) – mimic

neurotransmitter and decrease serotonin transmission – decrease anxiety
- **psychostimulants**, e.g. caffeine (increase dopamine release), amphetamine (increase dopamine release), cocaine (prevents dopamine reuptake) – increased arousal, euphoria
- **anti-psychotic agents** (neuroleptics), e.g. chlorpomazine – blocks dopamine receptors
- **mood stabilisers**, e.g. lithium salts – decrease release of noradrenalin and serotonin
- **hallucinogens,** e.g. LSD (blocks serotonin receptors), cannabis (release of noradrenalin)
- **narcotic agents** (opiods), e.g. heroin, morphine – increase endorphins and enkephalins – pain relief and euphoria
- **neurological drugs**, e.g. local anaesthetics (inhibit movement of sodium ions and action potential – no pain or movement possible), analgesics (e.g. aspirin) (block pain receptors).

Questions

Test yourself – then check your answers.

Section 1

1. Name the various regions of the forebrain, midbrain and hindbrain.
2. What is the function of the autonomic nervous system?
3. How does the endocrine system function?
4. How can the CNS, ANS and endocrine systems affect physiological funtioning?
5. What effects on behaviour can be caused by the CNS, ANS and endocrine systems?
6. Explain how a nerve impulse is propagated.
7. Explain how information is transmitted across a synapse.
8. Explain the mechanisms involved in the effects of psychoactive drugs.
9. What are the classifications of psychoactive drugs? Give examples.

2 | Cortical functions

2.1 Methods and techniques used to investigate cortical functioning

Electrical stimulation

Some methods are more accurate than others.

- electrodes used to electrically stimulate small regions of brain in conscious patient – behaviour/experience recorded
- e.g. Penfield ('58) stimulation of **temporal lobe** – vivid memories recorded
- stimulation of **visual cortex** – flashing lights, **auditory cortex** – sounds sensed
- can be used to identify regions associated with particular functions.

Chemical stimulation
- use of drugs to **stimulate or block specific neurotransmitters** – behaviour recorded
- e.g. stimulate/inhibit dopamine pathways – investigation of psychosis – schizophrenia
- e.g. Grossman ('64) noradrenalin in rat brain – feeding observed
- difficult to determine precise effects and problems extrapolating from animal studies.

Deliberate physical damage
- **lesions** – severing connections in brain – now use heated electrode rather than knife
- e.g. Lashley ('29) lesions in regions of rat cortex – learning regions spread out
- **ablations** – removal/destruction of brain tissue
- e.g. original lobotomy – destruction/removal of frontal lobes
- **neurotoxins** – destroy neurones using specific neurotransmitter
- **destructive techniques** so irreversible effects and damage to brain may be widespread
- animals often used – cannot necessarily relate to humans.

Illness or accidental damage

- **post-mortem** examination of brains of patients with problems
- e.g. schizophrenics' brains 6% lighter than normal
- **tumours** in brain can be localised using PET scan, behaviour noted
- **brain damage due to head injury**, e.g. Phineas Gage, severe damage to frontal lobes, became less inhibited, e.g. Grafman et al. ('86) brain damaged soldiers – reduced IQs
- difficult to compare before and after – before is usually retrospective account
- behaviour may be altered due to trauma of injury or illness.

Non-invasive techniques

Accurate and safe – but expensive and time-consuming.

- **EEG (electroencephalograph)** – electrodes on surface of skull detect electrical activity of brain when presented with stimuli or carrying out activities
- **CAT (computed axial tomography) scan** – many X-ray pictures put together by computer
- **PET (positron emission tomography) scan** – radioactive glucose injected into patient, active regions take up more – show up more on scan (detects radioactivity)
- **MRI (magnetic resonance imaging)** – head in magnetic field, radiowaves used to generate 3D picture of brain structure
- **non-invasive** so no long term effects (radioactivity doses for PET are very small).

2.2 Research into localisation of function in the brain

Sensory processes

Interpretation of sensory information.

- **contralateralisation** – left hemisphere receives sensory info. from right side of body several regions of cortex associated with sensory functions: **visual cortex** (occipital lobe); **auditory cortex** (temporal lobe); **somatosensory cortex** (just behind motor cortex)
- these **primary** sensory cortical regions send info. to **secondary (and tertiary)** cortical regions for **interpretation of sensory information = perception**.

Motor processes

Control of movement.

- **contralateralisation** – left hemisphere controls movement of right side of body
- **motor cortex** is band across top of brain
- sub-regions control movement of different parts of the body – size of brain region related to intricacy of control of movement, e.g. large region for hands
- **cerebellum** also important for fine coordination of movements.

Language

- **Broca's area – production of speech** – left cortex only – damage to this region results in motor aphasia – inability to produce speech
- **Wernicke's area – speech comprehension** – left cortex only – damage to this region results in receptive aphasia – cannot understand speech
- **left-handedness** may be problem for writing since language centres on left, left hand controlled by right brain.

Hemisphere asymmetries and the split brain

The 2 hemispheres are not identical.

- hemisphere **asymmetry** seen in language regions of brain (on left)
- **motor and sensory** regions do not show asymmetry – are bilateral
- **hemisphere dominance** – 90% people have dominant left hemisphere, so are right handed
- **stuttering and dyslexia** associated with mixed dominance – neither completely dominant
- Rasmussen and Milner ('77) **right** hemisphere associated with visuo-spatial tasks and emotional expression and understanding, **left** associated with language and analytical skills.

Split brain studies
- corpus callosum connects 2 cerebral hemispheres – sever this = **split brain**
- e.g. Sperry ('61) found differences in spatial and analytical abilities of 2 hemispheres – words presented to right hemisphere only (left visual field) cannot be read
- e.g. Sperry and Gazzaniga ('67) word in left visual field (right cortex) – could not say word but could pick up correct object with left hand (controlled by right cortex)
- **problems** – patients suffered from epilepsy – brains may not be typical
- patients adapt to split brain rapidly – generate methods of communication.

Neural plasticity
- if brain is damaged, **new pathways** can be set up and other regions can perform functions
- e.g. damage to left cortex of child – language centres develop in right cortex
- Gooch ('80) removal of left hemisphere, language skills returned (very slowly) to near normal levels of functioning – high plasticity.

2.3 Neurophysiological basis of visual perception

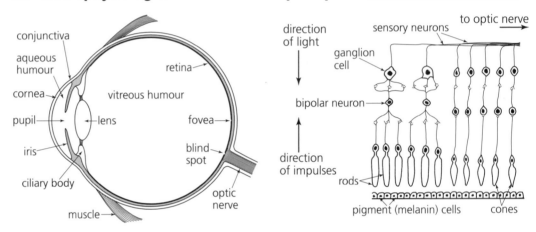

Figure 3.2 Structure of the eye   Figure 3.3 Structure of the retina

Sensation occurs in the eye – organisation of information starts.

Processes in the eye
- **light** (amount controlled by iris) passes through conjuctiva, cornea (initial refraction), aqueous humour, lens (refracts light), vitreous humour to retina
- **accommodation – lens shape altered** to focus light on fovea – distant object, less refraction needed, flatter lens (ciliary muscles relaxed) and vice versa
- **retina** covers inside of eyeball = **photoreceptor cells** – cones concentrated at fovea (centre of visual field), rods over rest of retina
- **rods** (125 million) detect light/dark, sensitive in low light levels, low acuity
- **cones** (6 million) detect colour, function in bright light only (low sensitivity), high acuity
- three types of cone – sensitive to long (red), medium (green), short (blue) wavelength light
- sensitivity and acuity explained by connections to bipolar and ganglion cells
- each cone connects to **one or two bipolar** cells only (difficult to stimulate – only in bright light, but each cell represents small region of retina)
- **several rods** connect to 1 bipolar cell (summation, easier to stimulate, but large region of retina covered)
- **after images** occur due to 'tiring' of photoreceptors – slow firing rate with constant exposure.

From eye to brain
- **optic nerves** from both eyes meet at **optic chiasma** – some nerve fibres cross over
- nerve fibres from **left** hand side of both retinas (right visual field) travel to **visual cortex of left cerebral hemisphere** via lateral geniculate nucleus of the thalamus (and vice versa)
- **each hemisphere** receives info. from **both eyes**, of same part of visual field – greater

disparity the further the object – **depth perception**
- visual cortex reassembles 'dots' of information from photoreceptors – **interpretation as shapes and objects = perception**
- Hubel and Wiesel ('62) simple, complex and hypercomplex cells in visual cortex of cat – arranged in functional columns – shows reintegration of information – bottom-up process
- cortical cells responding to orientation of lines develop (or are maintained) through experience (Blakemore and Mitchell ('73) cats in vertical world – not perceive horizontal)
- **colour perception** due to three types of cones, stimulated by specific wavelengths of light. **Opponent process coding** occurs initially via cones, bipolar and ganglion cells. **Trichromatic theory** explains perception of precise colour – specific wavelength stimulates 3 types of cone in particular pattern – integration occurs in visual cortex.

More organisation of information leading to interpretation = perception.

Section 2

Questions

Test yourself – then check your answers.

1. List the methods used to study cortical functioning.
2. What are the advantages and disadvantages of deliberate physical damage?
3. What are the advantages and disadvantages of non-invasive techniques?
4. Which regions of the brain are associated with sensory and motor processes?
5. Where are the main language centres in the brain?
6. Explain the findings of split brain studies.
7. What evidence is there for neural plasticity?
8. Describe the visual processes occurring in the eye.
9. What processes occur for visual information to be interpreted by the brain?
10. Explain how we perceive colour.

3 Awareness

3.1 Bodily rhythms and states of awareness

Bodily rhythms

- **bodily rhythms = cyclic activity** – can be controlled internally – by an internal clock (pacemaker), e.g. squirrels hibernate at the correct time of year even if the temperature and light/dark regime remain constant
- **pacemaker = innate, internal clock** – e.g. pineal gland of birds and reptiles generates rhythmic changes in melatonin production (more melatonin, decreased arousal)
- bodily rhythms may be controlled by external rhythmic activity – **zeitgebers (time-givers)** – e.g. daylength, temperature, lunar cycle, tidal rhythm
- **types of rhythm: circadian** = about 24 hours, e.g. human sleep/wake, **ultradian** = <24 hours, e.g. breathing, **infradian** = >24hrs, e.g. seasonal cycles – hibernation, mating.

Evidence for bodily rhythms

Humans have a diurnal rythm.

- Aschoff ('65) participants in cave for weeks in constant environment – 25 hour cycle
- seems internal pacemaker not set at precisely 24 hours, zeitgebers used to reset daily
- **individual differences** – Aschoff and Wever ('76) some show 29 hr wake, 21 hr sleep
- **body temperature** has precise 24 hr cycle – lowest at 4am, back to normal by 8am
- increased motor accidents between midnight and 6am (Horne ('92))
- **effects on shift work**: zeitgeber has not changed, less sleep gained if sleep during day, also low temperature at 4am and **low cognitive functioning** (Folkard et al. ('93) industrial accidents could be caused)

- **effects of jet lag** – similar to shift work – easier to shift to later time zone and increase rhythm
- **menstrual cycle** – internal control by hormones, can be affected by pheromones (zeitgeber)
- **seasonal affective disorder (SAD)** – lack of daylight in winter associated with depression.

States of awareness

- Oakley ('85) three levels of awareness:
  simple awareness – reflexes, classical conditioning, only sub-cortical brain regions required;
  consciousness – memory, complex learning, cortex and limbic system required;
  self-awareness – aware of existence of self, highly developed cortex required (higher primates) – red spot and mirror test (self-recognition)
- Freud distinguished between conscious and unconscious mind
- **conscious** = what we are aware of
- **pre-conscious** (subconscious) = edge of awareness, can be brought into consciousness
- **unconscious** = repressed information, not aware of its existence
- **altered states of awareness** – brain patterns can be affected in number of ways:
  i. **drugs** – e.g. LSD can produce loss of self-awareness and hallucinations
  ii. **psychosis** – schizophrenia, manic-depression – loss of self-awareness and hallucinations.

Sleep and dream states
sleep is altered state of awareness

- several stages of awareness when going to sleep, studied using EEG:
  stage 0 – relaxed, **awake** – alpha waves 8–12 Hz
  stage 1 – **transition** from wake to sleep, high frequency, low amplitude, desynchronised waves
  stage 2 – **deeper sleep** – alpha waves with sleep spindles and k-complexes
  stage 3 – **even deeper sleep** – low frequency (1–2 Hz) delta waves for about half of EEG, no spindles, reduced body activity, e.g. low temperature
  stage 4 – **very deep sleep**, very difficult to wake, more than half EEG consists of delta waves, lasts about half hour
- **REM** (rapid eye movement) sleep – **paradoxical** sleep – difficult to wake but electrical activity of brain irregular, similar to awake – associated with dreaming
- alternate through sleep stages throughout night – enter stages in succession then cycle
- Meddis ('79) distinction between REM and NREM sleep – **REM** = increased heart rate and metabolic rate, voluntary muscles cannot move, **NREM** = opposite.

3.2 Nature and functions of sleep

Nature of sleep

- stages of sleep as described above
- sleep/wake cycle follows **circadian rhythm** – pineal gland involved – darkness induces melatonin production, induces serotonin production in raphe nuclei (near pons varioli), affects RAS which controls transition between sleep and wake
- **factor S** – accumulates in brain during day, associated with drowsiness
- Jouvet ('67) locus coeruleus (region of pons) linked with REM sleep
- sleep deprivation studies – Webb and Bonnet ('79)
  i. **no major effects** of only 2 hr sleep on 1 night,
  ii. **gradual reduction** from 8–4 hrs sleep has no effect,
  iii. **sudden change in amount** of sleep leads to irritability, fatigue and impaired cognitive functioning

iv. lack of REM sleep (but normal NREM) produces same results, but REM rebound

v. when gradual reduction of sleep, amount of REM remains constant at about two hrs

- Jouvet ('67) REM deprivation – cats on 'islands', slip into water when REM sleep – hypersexuality observed and eventually death – shows importance of REM sleep.

Theories of sleep

2 main theories of sleep.

Restoration theory (Oswald ('66))

- sleep is for restoration and replenishing
- Shapiro et al. ('81) marathon runners required extra sleep – but Horne and Minard ('85) found no link between activity levels and amount of sleep
- **REM sleep restores and replenishes brain**, e.g. stimulates protein synthesis
- **NREM sleep restores and replenishes body** – stage 4 important for release of growth hormone and stimulation of protein synthesis (fibrosistis sufferers have less stage 4 sleep)
- infants have rapid growth, have much more sleep and more REM sleep (50%)
- nb – REM sleep is extremely active – does not match with restoration idea.

Evolutionary theory (Meddis ('75))

- **evolutionary advantage** to sleeping
- remain still and hidden from predators, less likely to be found, more likely to survive and pass on genes to next generation – also energy is conserved by remaining still
- Lloyd et al. ('84) species vary in amount of sleeping – if lack of safe hiding places or great risk from predators or if need to feed for long time have little sleep, e.g. cow
- **infant sleeping behaviour** – less likely to attract attention of predator if asleep – more time for parents to find food (prevents exhaustion)
- but – all mammals sleep, only the amount varies – must serve another function
- Empson ('89) sleep must be vital since prolonged deprivation can lead to death – not just hiding from predators.

Summary

- sleep is a **basic biological need** – lack of sleep results in death
- **REM sleep** is the **most important part of sleep** (Jouvet ('67))
- Horne ('88) core sleep = essential, supplemented by optional sleep (for energy conservation or hiding)
- different sleeping patterns have evolved depending on lifestyle and habitat.

Theories of dreaming

1 **Freud** – dreamwork **disguises latent content of dreams to manifest content** – less stress on conscious mind from dealing with repressed desires

2 **cognitive restoration** (Crick and Mitchison ('83)) – reorganisation of inputs, removal of unwanted information – random generation of impulses to test linkages results in dreams

3 **making sense of experiences** (Evans ('84)) – sort through inputs from day and link to past experiences – may result in problem-solving.

3.3 Hypnotic states

Nature of hypnotic state

Various features associated with hypnotic state.

Susceptibility

individual differences in susceptibility to hypnosis have been observed – can be tested using **Stanford Hypnotic Susceptibility Scale** (12 items) – 5–10% population = highly resistant, 15% = highly sensitive (have positive attitudes to hypnosis, more imaginative (McIlveen ('95)).

Memory

suggested that **memory recall is improved** under hypnosis – conflicting evidence, e.g. Orne ('51) showed increased confabulation in hypnotic state – see practical applications below.

Pain

susceptible individuals **claim not to feel pain** while in hypnotic state – they do show grimacing Bakal ('79) – cold pressor test – hypnotised individuals can stand extreme cold for longer.

Trance logic

hypnotised and non-hypnotised individuals **behave in different ways** – fewer non-hypnotised respond to post-hypnotic suggestion (Orne et al. ('68)).

Theories of hypnosis

Altered state of consciousness

- hypnotic state is **qualitatively different** from non-hypnotic
- Hilgard ('77) **dissociation model** – consciousness is split into several, dissociated parts – each can be separated from consciousness, e.g. pain is removed from consciousness
- explains 'hidden observer' = remaining conscious part – cold pressor test
- difficult to test and disprove – brain activity is not different in hypnotised and non-hypnotised.

Non-state theory

- hypnosis is not a different state of consciousness and can be explained using **normal psychological theory**
- demand characteristics – participant expects to behave in certain way and complies
- Barber ('79) hypnotic state is **role-playing** by participants, based on **role expectations**, **experimenter bias**, **demand characteristics** and possibly **social pressure**
- cannot explain 'hidden observer' or pain-relief in hypnosis.

Practical applications of hypnosis

Recall of memories

- suggestion that memory **recall improved** under hypnosis – useful for eye-witness testimony
- problems – memories may be **confabulated** – **unconsciously altered** but recalled as if fact – information may be added or removed – leading questions have greater effect
- **false confidence** in memories recalled under hypnosis – misleading for juries.

Regression

- recall of **repressed memories** from childhood
- same problems as above – **confabulation** – **false memory syndrome**
- leading questions by psychotherapist can lead to generation of **false memories** which are then considered to be real by the patient
- **difficult to validate** recovered memories – retrospective.

Analgesia

- hypnosis can **increase pain tolerance**
- useful, and used, in **childbirth**, **dentistry**, even **surgery**
- mechanism for pain relief is unknown.

Behaviour change

- hypnosis has been used in attempt to **alter behaviour**, e.g. giving up smoking
- positive effects seen may be due to **expectations and social support**.

Section 3

1. How are bodily rhythms controlled?
2. What evidence is there for the existence of bodily rhythms in humans?
3. List the different states of awareness.
4. Describe the different states within the sleep state.
5. What are the effects of sleep deprivation?
6. What are the assumptions of the restoration theory of sleep?
7. Provide evidence for and against the restoration theory of sleep.
8. What evidence is there for the evolutionary theory of sleep?
9. What are the effects of the hypnotic state?
10. Outline the 2 types of theories of hypnosis.
11. What are the practical applications of hypnosis?

Test yourself –
then check
your answers.

4 | Motivation, emotion and stress

Motivation and emotion shape and direct our behaviours. **Motivation** drives us to achieve a goal, **emotions** are specific arousal states which can affect our motivation.

4.1 Relationship between brain and motivation and emotion

- several approaches and theories attempting to explain motivation and emotion, e.g. behaviourist, psychoanalytic, humanistic, cognitive, neurobiological
- vary in importance placed on brain in motivation and emotion.

Motivation

The brain affects motivation.

- **homeostatic drive theory** involves hypothalamus (part of brain) as sensor – detecting changes in blood, and affecting behaviour accordingly via somatic nervous system
- **feeding regulatory centre** (ventro-medial nucleus) in hypothalamus – damage to this area results in massive overeating and weight gain (hyperphagia) by rats (Teitelbaum ('67))
- damage to lateral hypothalamus inhibits feeding (aphagia) and leads to starvation
- possible that lesions in vmn reduces sensitivity to internal cues (e.g. blood sugar/fat) so over-reliant on external cues (taste of food)
- oversimplistic – hypothalamus cannot be only factor in eating behaviour
- concentration of salts in blood detected by **volume and osmoreceptors** in hypothalamus, induces drinking behaviour (and release of ADH, increases water retention of kidneys)
- but – drinking stops before blood is altered – stomach distension may be involved
- **drive reduction theory** uses conditioning techniques to explain motivation (see below)
- S–R links build up in brain – relationship with motivation.

Emotion

Brain regions affect emotions.

- **Papez-Maclean limbic theory** – limbic system – **hypothalamus** and **thalamus** associated with sex drive, pleasure and aggression – **amygdala** and **hippocampus** associated with self-preservation – **cingulate gyrus** associated with pleasure and sexual behaviour
- cerebral cortex – removal of cortex of cat resulted in sham rage (Bard ('29)) – prevented if hypothalamus removed – cortex assoc. with aggression and hypothalamus necessary?
- but – stimulation of human hypothalamus has no emotional effect (Jacobson ('68))

- frontal lobes – removal of these in chimpanzee results in docility
- **right cerebral hemisphere** associated with emotional interpretation and negative mood (affect) expression in humans.

Importance of brain in main theories (in more detail below):

- **James-Lange theory** – external stimulus perceived by cerebral cortex, affects autonomic n.s. and peripheral n.s. – physiological changes, feedback from bodily changes via thalamus – changes interpreted as emotion by cortex
- **Cannon-Bard theory** – emotion-arousing stimulus perceived, processed by thalamus, cortex generates emotion (physiological changes occur in parallel)
- **Cognitive labelling theory** – extension of James-Lange – interpretation of physiological changes depends on cause of changes – determined by cognition (brain) – cognitive appraisal theory is extension.

4.2 Theories of motivation and emotion

Motivation

Physiological

Homeostatic drive theory
- maintenance of **constant internal environment** is vital
- tissue needs lead to internal imbalances, lead to homeostatic drives, lead to changes in behaviour, lead to restoration of balance
- Cannon and Washburn ('12) correlation between stomach contractions and hunger pangs
- but – removal of stomach, hunger still occurs – hunger can occur with full stomach
- internal imbalance of sugar/fat detected by ventro-medial nucleus of hypothalamus
- hypothalamus has osmoreceptors – control of drinking (see Section 4.1)
- **only explains primary, biological drives**.

Drive reduction theory (Hull ('43))
- **need = physiological, drive = psychological**
- primary, physiological need reduced by drive reducing behaviour = positive reinforcement
- learning occurs – drive reducing behaviour is reinforced
- but – drive (e.g. to feed) can occur without need (e.g. for food)
- cannot explain latent learning – learning without reinforcement or drive reduction
- **only considers primary drives** – limited, particularly for human behaviours.

Non-physiological

Needs theories
- humanist theories consider **importance of non-physiological drives**
- Murray ('38) listed 20 human motives/needs including dominance, achievement, autonomy, affiliation, nurturance, understanding
- McClelland ('61) need for achievement (nAch) as motivator
- Rogers' theory centres on positive regard and self-actualisation
- Rubin and McNeil ('83) motives classified into 3 types: survival/physiological; competence/cognitive; social motives.

Maslow's hierarchy of needs
- Maslow ('54) separated needs into physiological and self-actualisation needs
- needs can be arranged hierarchically – (lowest) physiological; safety; love and belonging; esteem; cognitive; aesthetic; self-actualisation (highest)
- lowest needs must be satisfied first, then move up hierarchy to attempt to satisfy next
- lowest generate strongest drives and most easy to satisfy
- **little scientific evidence** – difficult to test
- hierarchy may not be strictly followed (e.g. ignore safety needs in dangerous sports).

2 physiological theories of motivation.

2 non-physiological theories of motivation.

Emotion

Theories of emotion indicate a **link between physiological and psychological factors** although the emphasis varies from theory to theory.

4 main theories of emotion.

James-Lange theory
- perception of **stimulus** causes bodily changes (e.g. increased adrenalin and running), these are fed back to cortex of brain via thalamus and interpreted as emotion
- Laird ('74) cartoons rated as funnier if facial muscles in 'smiling' position
- there are physiological differences between different primary emotional states (e.g. Ekman et al. ('83)) – but is this true for all the subtle emotional variants?
- some evidence shows physiological changes do not generate emotions (Cannon-Bard theory).

Cannon-Bard theory
- **physiological** changes and **emotions** both occur **independently and in parallel** as a result of the stimulus
- Marañon ('24) adrenalin injections gave physiological effects only – '**as if**' emotions
- Valins ('66) fake heart rates given to men looking at female models, rate as more attractive if think heart rate higher – not consciously aware of real heart rate
- Hohmann ('66) damage to spinal cord – emotions affected
- cannot explain the 'as if' emotions.

Cognitive factors used to interpret physiological state.

Cognitive labelling theory
- **perception of stimulus** leads to **physiological changes** and **awareness of arousal** (via thalamus, to cortex), **cognition used to interpret** arousal as emotion
- Schachter and Singer ('62) four groups – adrenalin and placebo injections, those aware of arousal caused by injection (or not aroused) less likely to join in emotional
- physiological arousal necessary (placebo group did not join in)
- Dutton and Aron ('74) 'love on a suspension bridge' – mislabelling of arousal
- **emotions can arise without cognition** – e.g. perceptual defence of subliminal words.

Alter cognitive appraisal
↓
alter physiological changes
↓
alter emotions.

Cognitive appraisal theory (Lazarus ('82))
- **extension of cognitive labelling** theory
- **difference =** some cognitive processing must occur before a physiological reaction to a stimulus can occur – further analysis of changes and situation occurs – emotion felt
- Schachter and Singer ('62) level of arousal depends on cognitive appraisal of event
- but – Zajonc ('84) emotional response can precede cognitive processing.

4.3 Physiological effects of stress

- stress responses occur as a **reaction** to events which are perceived as physically or psychologically **threatening**
- the physiological responses are often referred to as the '**fight or flight**' response – the hormonal aspect is known as the **pituitary-adrenal stress syndrome**.

Short-term response = fight or flight
- **response to stressor** – hypothalamus stimulates pituitary to secrete ACTH – stimulates adrenal cortex to secrete stress hormones (e.g. adrenalin) – produce changes in the body
- **in addition** – hypothalamus stimulates sympathetic nervous system which causes adrenal medulla to secrete adrenalin and causes activation of other glands and smooth muscles
- **many changes** in body occur – increased **blood sugar**, increased **heart rate and blood pressure**, blood vessels **constricted** around gut and near skin, **more blood sent to brain and muscles**, increased **breathing rate** – combine to provide **increased food and oxygen** for cells of brain and muscles.

Effective against physical danger (e.g. predator) but **not** useful against exam stress.

Long term effects
Selye ('79) prolonged exposure to a stressor can lead to a number of long-term effects

(elevated adrenalin, stomach ulcers, low white blood cells) – 3 stages in **general adaptation syndrome** (GAS):

1. **alarm** = 'fight or flight' response as described above
2. **resistance** = high levels of adrenalin but body 'tries' to return to normal
3. **exhaustion** = energy depletion, unable to maintain 'fight or flight'

- **susceptibility to disease** – chronic stress can lead to **high blood pressure**, **heart disease**, **ulcers** and generally **lowered immune response**
- stress can have direct negative effect on health (Karasek et al. ('81))
- Kielcolt-Glaser et al. ('87) poorer immune functioning in recently divorced/separated
- Schleifer et al. ('79) impaired immune systems in widowers of breast cancer victims
- Jemmot et al. ('85) students have low antibody counts for respiratory infection during exams
- Weiss ('72) predictable stressor, less illness in executive rats
- immune system and nervous system are connected (complex mechanism)
- **individual differences** in response to stress – **vulnerability-stress model**
- **biological predisposition** is inherited, effects (illness) only seen if encounter stressor
- individuals **respond differently** to stressors since have **different predispositions**.

More problems in low control situations.

4.4 Reduction of stress

Problem-focused strategies – deal with cause of stress
- first **define problem**, then **generate solutions** – choose the best
- may be **removal** of stressor or **avoidance** of stressor
- **control** – lack of control increases negative effects of stressor – Rotter ('66) **internal locus of control** results in less stress than external
- control of stressor may be gained by more effective **time management**
- **internal change** – may be unattainable goals causing stress.

Direct action.

Emotion-focused strategies – deal with negative emotions
- Kielcolt-Glaser et al. ('85) **relaxation** techniques reduce decline in immune functioning
- **biofeedback** – learn to control autonomic functions (e.g. heart rate) using feedback from monitors – time-consuming, costly
- **assertiveness training** – may then enable to take control of situation
- Moos ('88) seek **social support** from friends, do **exercise**, **vent anger**
- **anti-anxiety drugs**, e.g. Valium – problem with physical dependency
- Nolen-Hoeksema ('91) **distraction** produces relief from depression.

Indirect action.

Questions

Section 4

1. List the ways in which the brain can affect motivation.
2. Which regions of the brain are important for motivation? Give examples.
3. List the ways in which the brain can affect emotion.
4. Which regions of the brain are important for emotion? Give examples.
5. What are the main theories of motivation?
6. Outline 2 contrasting theories of motivation.
7. What are the main theories of emotion?
8. Give evidence for and against the cognitive labelling theory.
9. List the short-term effects of stress.
10. List the long-term effects of stress.
11. How may individual differences play a part in the long-term stress response?
12. List the problem-focused strategies for stress reduction.
13. List the emotion-focused strategies for stress-reduction.

Test yourself – then check your answers.

Chapter four

Atypical development and abnormal behaviour

1 Atypical development

1.1 Learning difficulties

What are learning difficulties?

- usually defined in terms of **IQ score**
- American Association on Mental Deficiency – IQ <70
- 95% children score 70–130 – 2½% <70 – definition based on statistics, not individuals (although individuals scoring <70 will face difficulties)
- sub-divisions: profound (<25); severe (25–39); moderate (40–54); mild (55–69)
- terms used to describe individuals with learning difficulties have changed over years – terms have negative connotations.

Causes of learning difficulties

Genetic (intrinsic) causes

Nature...

- many genetic disorders caused by **recessive genes** – must have two copies to exhibit disorder
- both parents must be carriers of gene – 1 in 4 chance of child having disorder
- e.g. **phenylketonuria (PKU)** – inability to metabolise phenylalanine, builds up, causes brain damage – effects can be greatly reduced with diet – blood tests of infants aid early detection
- e.g. **Down's syndrome** – extra chromosome 21 (3 copies) – 2 copies inherited from 1 parent (faulty cell division) – stimulating environments reduce effects
- e.g. **fragile X syndrome** – developmental delays experienced.

Environmental (extrinsic) causes

...or nurture?

- **prenatal influences** (teratogens) – e.g. rubella during 4–6th week of pregnancy causes damage to CNS, heart and hearing, e.g. drugs and alcohol, e.g. prenatal anoxia (lack of oxygen) causes low birth weight and associated with lower cognitive development
- **diet – vitamins** associated with IQ gains (Benton and Cook ('91))
- **physical damage** to brain, possibly by disease, e.g. encephalitis
- **environmental stimulation** will affect, but only up to a limit.

Problems associated with learning difficulties

Labelling

- can generate **negative stereotype** – lowered expectations of teacher – self-fulfilling prophecy – shown to occur (Rosenthal ('85)) – peers respond differently too.

Schooling – mainstream vs specialist

- **specialist schools** – expertise but lower expectations, lack of contact with other peers
- **mainstream schools** – more social and cognitive stimulation, increased contact – should reduce prejudice, but Abrams et al. ('90) found had little effect
- in general, movement away from specialist schools to integration in mainstream
- **statementing** (1981 Education Act) aims to provide resources for individual children with specific, statemented difficulties so they can attend mainstream schools.

Remedial schemes

- extra help with, e.g. language/reading – not always productive – can result in high expectations which can never be reached.

1.2 Physical and sensory handicaps

Definitions

- 'disability" now used rather than 'handicap'
- **handicap** refers to effect on social roles, **disability** to effect on everyday activities.

a. Cerebral palsy (affects 0.2% population)

Severity and limbs affected vary.

- **damage to brain** usually due to **lack of oxygen** (prenatal, during birth or early infancy), also by **bleeding** on brain, **jaundice**, **injury**
- **damage to motor cortex** – affects movement – only 50% walking by 5 yrs
- **damage to other cortical areas** (varies) – possible sensory problems – Wilson ('70) 7% cannot speak, 25% speech production impaired
- some can overcome difficulties, e.g. Richard Boydell, unable to speak, given foot-operated typewriter aged 30 yrs, complex sentence production in nine days (Fourcin ('75)).

Additional problems may arise

- lack of **motor stimulation** may retard sensory and cognitive development
- if children **institutionalised** even less stimulation, and development further delayed
- **difficulty interacting** may lead to problems in social development and poor self-image
- **poor self-image** may result from frustration at persistent problems.

Treatments

- **conductive education** – Peto Institute, Hungary – emphasises motor coordination, intense physiotherapy – results are ambiguous
- alternative – **stimulation of muscle groups** – Margaret Rood
- individuals affected in different ways, will respond to different treatment.

b. Hearing impairment

- **different degrees** of hearing impairment – affects 0.2% children
- profound deafness in only 1% of these
- several causes – 3 main: **nerve deafness**; **conductive deafness**; **glue ear.**

Additional problems

- **difficulty reading** – Conrad ('79) less so if parents' hearing impaired too
- **cognitive impairment** – varied findings – Phelps and Branyan ('90) non-verbal IQ lower for pre-linguistically deaf – hearing impaired better at recognising faces (Bellugi et al. ('90))
- **social development** – may be impaired due to limited interactions.

Language

- **oral tradition** – use of hearing aids, lip reading, word production
- **sign language** – true, gestural languages – own grammar – e.g. ASL and BSL – Quigley and Paul ('87) good starting point for reading and writing
- Schlesinger and Meadows ('72) if hearing impaired child has hearing impaired parents, sign language picked up at similar rate to oral language – signing simplified (Motherese)
- **sign systems** – signs correspond with words in spoken language – easier to communicate with hearing – Quigley and Paul ('87) not good for reading and writing – slower system.

c. Visual impairment

- **varying degrees** of visual impairment – 0.01% children show statutory blindness
- causes: **disease** (e.g. prenatal rubella), **brain damage**, **congenital** disorder.

Additional problems
- **social development** – restricted inputs, no facial expressions including smiling, communication more difficult – Fraiberg ('77) emotional and social development suffers
- **reading** – braille is more difficult and slower than reading – poor substitute
- **cognitive development** – visual impairment affects sensory-motor development
- **delays in language acquisition** – prevented if given objects to manipulate (Fraiberg ('79))
- **speech production** – Mills ('87) visually impaired make more errors with sounds that have visibly different mouth movements.

Coping with physical and sensory handicaps

- **secondary handicaps** may result from primary (see additional problems above)
- **multiple handicaps** may occur – more difficult when combined
- **prejudice** – stereotypical images in media are not helpful
- **labelling** – issues mentioned above (in learning difficulties)
- **development of self** – lack of role models to identify with
- **individual differences** affect coping – finances, social support, age, personality, motivation
- **strategies** for coping: **information**, **control** situation, set achievable **goals**, find **help**.

1.3 Emotional disturbances and behavioural problems

Emotional and behavioural problems in children have a variety of causes.

a. Attention-deficit hyperactivity disorder (ADHD)

Characteristics
- inappropriate **hyperactivity**, poor sustained **attention**, **impulsiveness**
- affects more boys than girls, normal IQ but do not do well in classroom (disruptive).

Possible causes

- **biological** – Whalen ('89) minimal brain damage, so extra stimulation needed, underarousal – treatment with stimulants (e.g. Ritalin) reduces hyperactivity
- **overarousal** – attention switching
- **diet** – additives cause ADHD – controversial claim – treatment, e.g. Feingold diet (additive free) – may be placebo effect
- **parental behaviour** – but different parental responses are cued by differences in child's behaviour.

Treatments

- **stimulants** improve behaviour of 75% ADHD children, but only while taking drug long-term effects unknown, side effects = insomnia and appetite loss
- **behaviour therapy** – reinforcement system, effective in short term but behaviours become extinct when reinforcement stops – also, lack of generalisation.

b. Autism
rare condition – Gilberg ('90) 0.002% children, more likely in boys

Characteristics

- **uncommunicative**, lack of empathy, emotion and attachments
- **stereotypical**, repetitive behaviours
- **language problems** – lack of speech, repetitive or confusion of pronouns (you and I)
- **infantile autism** associated with low IQ scores (<70), but may have above average functioning in specific area, e.g. drawing, music, calculations, rote learning
- **Asperger's syndrome** (form of autism) associated with normal or high IQ
- **sensitivity** may be altered – heightened or lowered.

Nature...
...or nurture?

Possible causes
- **genetic** – links with fragile X, twin studies suggest genetic factors (Szatmari and Jones ('91))
- **biological** – some links with epilepsy, altered sensitivity – neurological problem
- **parental influence** – impersonal relationships (emotional refrigeration – Kanner ('43))
- **lack of personal intelligence** – Hobson ('86) unable to understand others' emotions
- **lack of Theory of Mind** (Leslie and Frith ('90)) – mind-blindness, inability to understand others – Baron-Cohen et al. ('85) many autistic fail false belief tasks.

Treatment
- **behaviour therapy** – use of reinforcement
- **play therapy**.

c. Developmental dyslexia (more likely in boys than girls)

Not all dyslexia is
the same.

Characteristics
- **disability does not match child's other abilities**
- **specific learning disability** of reading, spelling and writing
- **reversal and rotation of letters**; **syllable omission**; **losing track** while reading
- may have general **language problems** – speech disorder/acquisition problem
- **forgetfulness and clumsiness** associated with dyslexia (Fawcett ('94)).

Possible Causes
- developmental dyslexia has number of possible root causes
- **genetic factors** – possible sex-linkage since more likely in boys, twin studies support (Wadsworth et al. ('89))

Evidence for a
variety of causes.

- **minimal brain damage** – acquired and developmental similar characteristics – similar causes?
- **automaticity deficit** (Fawcett and Nicholson ('94)) – problem generating automatic tasks – could account for clumsiness as well as reading/writing problems
- **perceptual problems** cause visual memory problem
- **difficulty processing speech sounds** (phonemes) – e.g. Olsen et al. ('89) dyslexic more difficulty moving sounds in words, also slower reading words and non-words.

Treatment
structured multisensory method – use more than one sense to analyse new information, e.g. see, hear, say, feel – Hulme ('81) letter string memory better if traced.

Questions

Section 1

1. How are learning difficulties defined?

2. List the possible causes of learning difficulties.

3. What additional, social problems may be associated with learning difficulties?

4. What are the specific effects of cerebral palsy, and the additional problems that may arise?

Test yourself –
then check
your answers.

5. What additional problems may arise due to hearing impairment?

6. What additional factors may affect the ability to cope with physical and sensory handicaps?

7. What evidence is there for the various possible causes of ADHD?

8. How effective are the treatments for ADHD?

9. What are the characteristics of autism?

10. Evaluate the possible explanations for autism.

11. List the possible causes of dyslexia and assess their plausibility.

2 | Conceptions and models of abnormality

2.1 Definitions and classifications of normal and abnormal behaviours

Definitions

Deviation from the (statistical) norm
- in a normal distribution 95% population within 2 standard deviations of mean
- outside this range = abnormal.

Problems
- some abilities outside normal range are desirable, e.g. genius, extremely fast running speed
- not based on individual's behaviour or ability, only statistical.

5 types of definition – each has problems.

Deviation from the expected
- expect certain behaviours in certain situations, e.g. in restaurant
- if behaviour deviates greatly from this regularly, assume behaviour is abnormal.

Problems
- need to see behaviour in number of situations – time-consuming
- more useful for friends/relatives noticing change in behaviour and seeking help.

Deviation from social standards
- society sets standards of social behaviour, those breaking rules = deviant
- standards change over time, e.g. unmarried motherhood was considered deviant.

Problems
- present society defines deviance – politically powerful, restricts individuals
- Szasz ('72) 'madness' engineered to label those the majority do not approve of.

Deviation from mental health
- set standards for what is healthy mental condition, check if deviate from this
- Jahoda ('58) healthy = self-acceptance, autonomy, potential for growth and development, accurate perception of reality, positive interpersonal relations.

Problems
- very few healthy people on Jahoda's scale and cannot measure most of factors so subjective
- imposed etic – e.g. autonomy is not valued in all cultures.

Dysfunction and distress
- dysfunction – inability to function normally, e.g. cannot go to work
- depressed/anxious states may result in distress and dysfunction.

Problems
- distress observed in normal behaviours, e.g. grieving
- some abnormal behaviours do not involve distress.

Classification

Symptoms that occur together repeatedly are classified as **syndrome**
- syndrome classified as category of disorder if agreement among clinicians
- categories of disorders used in classification schemes.

ICD and DSM
ICD = International Classification of Diseases (by World Health Organisation)
ICD-10 ('93) is current revision.

Sample of ICD-10

category	examples
organic mental disorders	senile dementia, Alzheimer's
schizophrenia	catatonic, disorganised
neurotic, stress-related and somatoform	phobias, obsessive-compulsive
mood (affective) disorders	depression
disorders of psychological development	autism, developmental dyslexia

Learn a few examples.

DSM = Diagnostic and Statistical Manual of Mental Disorders (by American Psychiatric Association) – includes diagnostic criteria for use in clinical practice
DSM-IV ('94) is current revision
DSM assessment is multi-axial – five axes: classification of **clinical** disorders; classification of **personality** disorders/mental retardation; general **medical** conditions; **psychosocial** and **environmental** problems; **global assessment** of functioning scale.

DSM-IV categories

major category	examples
clinical disorders	mood disorders, sleep disorders, eating disorders, schizophrenia
personality disorders	paranoid personality disorder, obsessive-compulsive personality disorder
mental retardation	genetic, antenatal damage

Learn a few examples.

Practical problems and ethical implications

Classification system is useless if not reliable and valid
- **reliability** – consistency of diagnosis = generally poor – Beck et al. ('62) inter-rater reliability at chance level
- **validity** – predictive, concurrent, aetiological – are diagnoses valid, are they real? Heather ('76) diagnosis equally likely to result in same or different treatment, shows lack of validity
- **prestige effect** – diagnosis affected by other's diagnosis, particularly if prestigious
- Rosenhan ('70) sane arrived at mental hospital, only symptom = heard voices, all diagnosed with schizophrenia and admitted – psychiatrists' diagnoses are invalid.

labelling – affects behaviour of individual – may behave in appropriate manner (Scheff ('66)).
Labels have negative connotations and stick with individual when cured.
DSM labels disorder, not person – in practice, probably has little effect on way treated by peers.

Classification system is questionable.

2.2 Alternative paradigms in abnormal psychology

Medical
- **physical** cause of disorder, identify symptoms, diagnose disorder, treat somatically.

5 main approaches widely different viewpoints.

For	Against
• drugs can affect neurotransmitters and therefore brain activity	• Szasz ('72) generates fear in others – politically engineered
• research suggests genetic predisposition to certain disorders	• Heather ('76) applies to psychoses, but not neuroses
• general paresis caused by Syphilis bacterium	• no blame so no responsibility, professionals and drugs relied on
• individual not to blame for disorder	• ignores social factors

Behavioural
- abnormal behaviour learned via S–R links
- **reinforcement** (positive and negative) of behaviour important – **operant conditioning**
- **classical conditioning** involved in phobia development
- **behaviour therapy** – behaviours can undergo extinction.

For	Against
• classical conditioning can explain phobias	• much research with animals – relevance questioned
• behaviour therapy useful for some disorders	• only symptoms treated, not problem
• individual differences accounted for	• reductionist approach

Cognitive
- **maladaptive thought processes** (unconscious) result in maladaptive behaviour
- extension of behaviourist approach – include thinking between S and R
- treatment involves restructuring of thought processes to make them adaptive.

For	Against
• maladaptive thinking found with many disorders (Gustafson ('92))	• maladaptive thinking could be effect rather than cause
• no labelling of disorders	• individual to blame – social conditions ignored
• individual taken into account	• individual therapy – social support ignored
• therapies have proved successful	

Humanistic
- **low self-worth** due to lack of unconditional positive regard from others
- **incongruence** between ideal-self and actual-self may lead to maladjustment
- **treatment** = unconditional positive regard from therapist.

For	Against
• person-centred approach – individual situation taken into account	• self-cure may not be possible and treatment not being sought
• optimistic – focused on well-being	• unconditional positive regard – difficult for parents
• lack of labelling – no disorder classification	• self-actualisation is culture-specific

Learn some advantages and disadvantages for each approach.

Psychodynamic

- if conflict unresolved may cause problems later, e.g. fixation, phobia
- repression pushes events too traumatic too deal with (at present) into unconscious – can affect behaviour later
- treatment involves **identifying and resolving unconscious, unresolved conflict**.

For	Against
• individuals with disorders often had traumatic events in childhood • no blame on individual – much on parents!	• difficult to analyse scientifically • reductionist model • treatment relies on expert help

2.3 Cultural and subcultural differences

Culture

- some disorders are **culturally relative** – only found in specific cultures, e.g. neurasthenia in China – do they only exist in specific cultures or is it diagnostic differences?
- many disorders vary in **frequency of diagnosis** in different cultures, e.g. British African-Caribbean up to seven times more likely to be diagnosed schizophrenic – possible reasons:
  i. **genetic effects** – more prevalent in specific group – not the case for schizophrenia
  ii. specific cultural groups encounter different amounts of stress due to **different social conditions** – stress linked with mental illness, e.g. schizophrenia
  iii. **cultural bias in diagnosis** – normality and abnormality defined in Western terms
  iv. persecution delusion may be real – discrimination – 'schizophrenia' may actually be acute stress reaction, results from social conditions (Littlewood and Lipsedge ('89)).

> Cultural differences may be due to differing environmental influences.

Gender

- some disorders more diagnosis in men (e.g. narcissistic personality disorder), some more in women (e.g. depression) – possible explanations:
  i. **genetic differences** – mixed evidence
  ii. **environment** – women experience a different environment to men, depression a response to situation – more likely to be abused, increased depression (Cochrane ('95))
  iii. **gender bias in diagnosis** – same symptoms, different gender, different diagnosis
  iv. female response to male-dominated world only abnormal since norm is male (Bem ('93)).

> Gender differences may be genetic, or environmental, or not real.

Social class

- lower SES associated with high incidence of mental disorders, several possible reasons:
  i. **higher stress levels** in lower SES groups, stress associated with mental illness
  ii. **coping resources** less accessible to lower SES – limited social support
  iii. **drift** – incidence equal in all groups, but those with disorders drift into lower status groups
  iv. **bias in diagnosis** – diagnosis and treatment affected by SES (Umbenhauer and DeWitte ('78)) – lower SES more serious, more hospitalisation, more physical treatment (Johnstone ('89)).

Questions

Section 2

1. List the definitions of normal and abnormal behaviours.

2. Give two problems for each of the definitions in question 1.

3. What is a syndrome?

4. Briefly outline the two main classification mechanisms.

5. What are the advantages of using classification systems?

6. What are the problems of classification systems?

7. What are the five alternative paradigms in abnormal psychology?

8. Give the advantages and disadvantages of the medical approach.

9. How does the cognitive approach explain abnormal behaviour?

10. What are the advantages and disadvantages of the humanistic approach?

11. Explain how culture can have an effect on the disorders recorded.

12. What are the explanations for different frequencies of disorders in men and women?

13. What is the association between social class and mental illness?

3 | Psychopathology

- there are many different mental disorders and many different explanations for them
- there are **two main types** of explanation: **genetic/neurological** and **social/psychological**
- **Diathesis-stress model** takes an interactionist view.

3.1 Schizophrenia

Description

- **loss of contact with reality** – NOT split personality
- out-dated classifications: Type I/functional/acute/positive vs Type II/organic/chronic/negative
- DSM-IV identifies three types: **paranoid**; **disorganised**; **catatonic**
- **three patterns of development** (about a third in each): **1. recovery** after only one or few episodes; **2. episodes throughout life** but function during remission periods; **3. deterioration**
- usual onset in females during twenties, males during teens/early twenties.

Explanations

Genetic/neurological

- **genetic predisposition** – much evidence to suggest genetic factors important – twin studies (e.g.Gottesman and Shields ('82)) and family studies (e.g. Kendler et al. ('85))
- **biochemical effects** – much evidence to suggest dopamine involved – L-dopa induces acute schizophrenic symptoms – drugs for control of schizophrenia inhibit dopamine
- but cannot say if dopamine causes symptoms or vice versa, or both caused by another
- **structural differences in brain** – schizophrenics have larger ventricles and lack asymmetry in amygdala
- **retrovirus** – viral, but assimilated into DNA (Crow ('84)).

Social/psychological

- **schizophrenogenic families** – Fromm-Reichmann ('48) outdated view that dysfunctional families cause schizophrenia – high emotional tension, close alliances and many secrets
- **double-bind situation** – Bateson et al. ('56) conflicting messages of care and criticism cause child to withdraw
- Laing ('59) **sane response** to insane environment
- effect on course of schizophrenia – Vaughn and Leff ('76) **expressed emotion (EE) hypothesis** – high EE interactions associated with relapse, more so without medication.

Diathesis-stress model
- **interaction** between genetic factors (good evidence) and environmental trigger – genetic predisposition, but not pre-determined, only high-risk.

3.2 Depression

affective (mood) disorder

Unipolar depression

Seligman

Description
- **reactive** depression – response to external events – short-term, severity varies
- **endogenous** depression – independent of external events, severe
- DSM-IV has two categories: **major depressive disorder (MDD) = severe**, often short-lived; **dysthymic disorder (DD) = chronic (long-term)** but less severe
- associated with a number of **symptoms** including: **low self-esteem**; **self-loathing**; **suicidal thoughts/attempts**; **loss of appetite**; **irritability**; **sadness**; **apathy**; **sleep disturbance**.

> More intense than "normal" depression.

Bipolar depression (manic-depressive psychosis)

Description
- **mood swings** between depression (symptoms as above) and mania (elation)
- mania **symptoms** include: **hallucinations**; **recklessness**; increased **energy**; increased **work/socialising**; more **talkative**; grandiose and persecutory **delusions**; **euphoria**
- moods may rapidly follow one another or have normal periods in between.

> Associated with creativity.

Explanations

Genetic/neurological
- **genetic predisposition** – twin studies (e.g. Price ('68)) suggest much more important for manic-depression than unipolar, same for family studies
- gene on chromosome 11 assoc. with manic-depression in Amish (Egeland et al. ('87))
- **biochemical** – problem with amine metabolism – three neurotransmitters: noradrenaline, serotonin, dopamine – but no evidence of low noradrenaline in depressed   *Schildkraut*
- **hormonal effects** – hormonal changes associated with depression (e.g. post-partum, pre-menstrual) but no differences found between depressed and non-depressed (Cooper ('88)).

> Nature...
> ...or nurture...
> ...or both?

Social/psychological
- **behaviourist** – learned helplessness (Seligman ('74)) may explain unipolar depression   *–Lewinsohn*
- **cognitive** – attribution of failure – internal/external; stable/unstable; global/specific – affects cognitive processing – internal, stable, global may lead to depression *Beck*
- **psychodynamic** – manic-depression is alternation of control by superego and ego
- **life events** – trigger for reactive depression (but not all depression).   *Bowlby*

Diathesis-stress model
- individual differences in susceptibility (tolerance levels) **interact** with environment.

3.3 Anxiety disorders

Phobias

Description
- **extreme, irrational fear** interfering with normal life
- DSM-IV identifies three types: **agoraphobia** (fear of open spaces); **social** phobias; **specific** (simple) phobias (e.g. arachnophobia (spiders), aerophobia (flying), xenophobia (strangers)).

Explanations

Genetic/neurological

- **genetic predisposition** to phobias – some support from twin studies comparing mono- (MZ) and dizygotic (DZ) twins, e.g. Torgersen ('83)
- **genetic – preparedness** to learn particular S–R links (Seligman ('71)) – e.g. phobias
- **neurological** – phobias associated with high arousal levels – but which causes which?

Social/psychological

- **behaviourist** – phobic item associated with fear (**classical conditioning**), then avoided and avoid anxiety (**operant conditioning**) – e.g. Watson and Raynor ('20) Little Albert
- **cognitive** – extension of behaviourist, including thinking – irrational thoughts about fearful situation lead to phobia (Beck ('63))
- **psychoanalytic** – original feared object/event is repressed – unconsciously fear displaced onto neutral – e.g. Freud ('09) Little Hans' – phobias more common in strict upbringings.

Diasthesis-stress model

- **interaction** between individual's anxiety tolerance level and environmental stress (individual tolerance level may be inherited, or via early experience).

Post-traumatic stress disorder (PTSD)

Description

- traumatic event leads to **traumatic stress disorder** (normal and temporary)
- some individuals continue to suffer after time = **PTSD**
- first in DSM in 1980, but known before, e.g. shell shock of First World War
- no evidence that any groups particularly susceptible to PTSD
- individual relives traumatic event – in dreams and flashbacks – avoids similar situations
- **lack of concentration**, **irritable**, **memory problems**, **increased anxiety**, **emotional distance**.

Explanations

Genetic/neurological

- affects **physiological stress response** – fight or flight – noradrenaline levels high in PTSD patients (Kosten et al. ('87)), may affect arousal levels
- eventual **noradrenaline depletion** may result in low motivation and poor memory.

Social/psychological

- **behaviourist** – items in environment associated with fear (from traumatic event) – environmental cues then elicit fear response – one-trial learning since very traumatic event
- **cognitive** – context-dependent memory – cues encoded at same time as traumatic memory – cues can trigger traumatic memory
- **cognitive** – perceived lack of control over events leads to irrational thought patterns
- **psychoanalytic** – traumatic event suppressed in unconscious mind – unconscious conflict continues as attempts to integrate.

Diathesis-stress model

- individuals have **different tolerance levels** so not all experience PTSD.

3.4 Eating disorders

Anorexia nervosa

Description

- **refusal to eat** (literally 'nervous loss of appetite' but not true) but pre-occupation with food
- **distorted body image** – perceive self as over-weight when under-weight

Nature...
...or nurture...
...or both?

Can occur immediately or with delay (can be years).

Nature...
...or nurture...
...or both?

10% of hospitalised cases die.

- **underweight**, **weak muscles**, **depression**, **lack of concentration**, **broken sleep**
- most common in 13–18 yr old females (affects 0.5–1%), associated with middle-class.

Bulimia nervosa

Description
- **binge eating** and **vomiting**/laxative use/fasting/exercise
- more likely to have **normal weight**
- **distorted body image**, can follow on from anorexia
- most common in females (1–5% 20+ yrs) – only few males.

Explanations for both disorders

Genetic/neurological
- **genetic predisposition** – evidence from twin studies (Holland et al. ('84))
- **hypothalamus** involved in maintenance of constant internal environment – can affect eating habits – malfunction could explain anorexia but no evidence yet. — *Keesey*

Social/psychological
- **behaviourist** – reinforcement of initial weight loss, likely to repeat dieting, further weight loss – attention can be reinforcement
- **psychoanalytic** – repression of sexual impulses, aim to regress to childhood (Bruch ('79))
- **psychoanalytic** – childhood sexual abuse repressed, leads to conflict at adolescence – expressed as eating disorder
- **humanistic** – exerting control over life – separate from parental control which dominates most of life – explains high incidence of anorexia in middle-class, where pressure to succeed.

Section 3

1. What are the main explanations for mental disorders?

2. What are the characteristics of schizophrenia?

3. What evidence is there for the genetic/neurological explanation of schizophrenia?

4. Describe the social/psychological explanation of schizophrenia.

5. How does the diathesis-stress model explain schizophrenia?

6. Distinguish between unipolar depression and manic-depressive psychosis (bipolar depression).

7. What are the genetic/neurological explanations of both forms of depression?

8. What are the social/psychological explanations of depression?

9. Outline the various explanations for phobias.

10. Describe the features of post-traumatic stress disorder.

11. Distinguish between anorexia and bulimia nervosa.

12. Outline the various explanations for eating disorders.

4 | Therapeutic approaches

4.1 Alternative types of treatment therapies

There is a wide variety of different therapeutic approaches: it is unlikely that any one therapy would ever be useful in treating all disorders.

Behaviour therapies

Classical conditioning techniques

Systematic desensitisation
- treatment of anxiety and phobias
- Wolpe ('58) – hierarchy of fear-inducing situations encountered with relaxation techniques.

Implosion therapy (flooding)
- treatment of anxiety and phobias
- remain with fear (real or imagined) – cannot maintain physiological fear response indefinitely, eventually tire and relax – new association built up – check health of patient first.

Aversion therapy
- treatment of addictions and habits
- association of unpleasant with neutral, e.g. vomiting (drug induced) associated with alcohol.

Operant conditioning techniques

Token economy
- positive reinforcement used for desirable behaviours, used in institutions
- tokens are secondary reinforcers – can buy primary reinforcers.

Modelling
- social learning theory – observation and imitation important
- behaviour of therapist observed, imitated, reinforced.

Social skills training
- extension of modelling
- role-play and feedback used (reinforcement) to shape behaviours.

For	Against
• very successful in treating phobias (e.g. McGrath et al. ('90), Craske and Barlow ('93)), anxieties, obsessive-compulsive disorders • relatively quick	• treatment of symptoms only • may be successful due to increased attention • ethics of behaviour modification

Cognitive-behavioural therapies

- rational-emotive therapy **(RET)** of Ellis ('62), later **REB(behavioural)T**
- **ABC** model used – **Activating** event, **Beliefs** about event, **Consequences** of beliefs (Ellis ('91)) – patient shown how maladaptive thought patterns lead to maladaptive behaviour
- **behavioural** element – role-play used to assess consequences of thought patterns.

For	Against
• much research shows effective for depression, anger, sexual problems and anti-social behaviour • as effective as drugs, lower relapse rate (Hollon et al. ('88))	• only treat thought patterns, not underlying causes • may only be suitable if good problem-solving skills • can lead to dependence on therapist

Treatment of phobias and addiction.

Behaviour shaping.

Altering thought.

Non-judgemental self-help.

Humanistic therapy

- **person-centred**, client-centred, widely used in counselling
- therapist shows **warmth** (unconditional positive regard), **genuineness** and **empathy**
- therapist is **non-judgmental**, **non-interventionist** – client generates own solution.

For	Against
• research shows effective, e.g. Rogers and Dymond ('54) • useful for wide range of problems, but not severe disorders	• difficult to analyse theoretically and scientifically • may require specific personality or cultural background to work

Psychodynamic approach

Resolution of unconscious conflicts.

- **unconscious conflicts** causing problem – bring to consciousness and resolve with therapist
- **free association**, **dream analysis** and **word association**
- **projective tests** – Rorschach Ink Blot, Thematic Apperception Test
- **transference** – patient may transfer repressed feelings onto therapist.

For	Against
• some studies show to be effective – but difficult to measure • play therapy developed for use with children	• focused on past, present problems ignored • long-term, time-consuming, expensive • only useful with intelligent and insightful • Eysenck ('52) less effective than no therapy

Somatic approach

Assumes biological basis for disorder, biological cure needed.

Chemotherapy (drugs)

Biological therapy.

- **biochemical basis** for disorder, can be treated chemically
- **three main types of drug**: anti-anxiety; antidepressant; anti-psychotic
- **anti-anxiety** – benzodiazepines, e.g. Valium – tolerance with long-term use
- **antidepressant** – monoamine oxidase inhibitors (toxic with some chemicals), tricyclics (side effects, e.g. mania), serotonin reuptake inhibitors, e.g. Prozac (side effects, e.g. nausea)
- **anti-psychotic** – lithium salts for manic-depression (side effects, e.g. convulsions), phenothiazines for schizophrenia (side effects, e.g. spasms, epileptic seizures).

For	Against
• very good evidence for effectiveness of all drugs, particularly anti-psychotic (other therapies little effect) • easy to administer (and prescribe) • fewer people institutionalised	• many side effects (including addiction) – do these outweigh benefits? • treat symptoms only – not cures, drug must continue to be taken or relapses occur • not effective for all patients

Electro-convulsive therapy (ECT)

Last resort treatment for severe depression.

- electrical current passed through brain – leads to seizure and convulsions
- thought to affect neurotransmitter levels, e.g. serotonin and dopamine – affect depression
- now only in non-dominant hemisphere and muscle relaxants and anaesthetic given first.

For	Against
• very effective treatment for severe depression – 60–70% improve	• relapses of depression occur
• no longer uncomfortable, few side effects with modern method	• precise mechanism for effectiveness not known
	• effective drugs available

Psychosurgery

Drastic therapy.

- **surgery on brain** to affect behaviour and personality
- **lobotomy, pre-frontal leukotomy, cingulotomy**.

For	Against
• can be effective in some cases, e.g. severe depression/anxiety (Beck and Cowley ('90))	• irreversible
	• effects variable and unpredictable
• available as last resort for those that might otherwise harm themselves (or others)	• lack of scientific understanding

4.2 Ethical issues in therapy and intervention

Defining abnormality

Issues associated with definition of abnormality.

There are a number of issues associated with defining an individual's behaviour as abnormal – some to do with the definition itself, others to do with implications of that definition.

  i. **labelling** – see Section 2.1
  ii. **diagnostic reliability and validity** – see Section 2.3
  iii. **diagnostic bias** (cultural, social, gender) – see Section 2.3
  iv. **necessity for identifying abnormality** – to protect the patient and others
  v. **issue of responsibility** – if labelled as mentally ill, responsibility removed from individual – if labelled as maladapted, patient is responsible for disorder, and for solving it
  vi. **criminal responsibility** – if found to be criminally insane, may be institutionalised indefinitely, rather than serve fixed term prison sentence – discourages this plea.

Rights of patient

Confidentiality

communication between patient and therapist is confidential – criminal activity is confidential, but if terrorism or child abuse, therapist must inform authorities.

Informed consent

ideally, patient informed about suitability, success rates and side effects of variety of therapies and takes active part in decision-making process – **informed consent not always possible** (may not fully understand, irrational judgement)

involuntary commitment – individuals can be institutionalised against their will = sectioning (due to Mental Health Act ('83)) – requires agreement of GP and one social worker

involuntary treatment – if sectioned, treatment is chosen by psychiatrist.

Abuse of power
psychiatrist seen as expert and powerful by patient – patients may start to take on beliefs of therapist – false memory syndrome (FMS) due to powerful suggestions from therapists? – sexual abuse, patients can believe they are in love with therapist (possibly due to transference), therapist must not take advantage but many instances recorded (Garrett and Davies ('94)).

Cultural issues
Eurocentric theories and practices not necessarily effective with all cultures – ideally, patients should be given option of own-culture therapist – Sue and Sue ('90) black patients have difficulty with white psychotherapists.

Deinstitutionalisation
- **release of patients into community** = deinstitutionalisation
- long-term institutionalised often lack social skills and ability to care for self – special training required prior to release
- community care required to follow up patients and check on medication (usually vital).

Mixed views of success of scheme.

Questions

Test yourself – then check your answers.

Section 4

1. List the types of therapeutic approaches.

2. What are the classical conditioning techniques? Give an example of their use.

3. What are the application of operant conditioning therapeutic techniques?

4. What are the advantages and disadvantages of the behaviour therapies?

5. Explain the reasoning behind cognitive-behavioural therapies.

6. How does humanistic therapy work?

7. What are the advantages and disadvantages of humanistic therapy?

8. Explain the psychodynamic approach to therapy.

9. List the types of somatic approach to therapy.

10. Provide arguments for and against one of the somatic approaches to therapy.

11. What ethical issues are associated with the definition of abnormality?

12. What issues about patients' rights have been brought to light?

13. What are the problems of informed consent?

14. Outline cultural issues of patients' rights.

15. What are the ethical issues surrounding deinstitutionalisation?

Chapter five

Cognitive psychology

1 Perceptual processes

1.1 Theories of perception

Hypothesis testing theory (Gregory, 1966)

Expectations and prior knowledge important for perception.

- **top-down processing** – **constructivist** approach – **concept-driven** processing
- **hypothesis** is generated about incoming visual information, this is tested
- **most probable explanation** is accepted
- **illusions** occur when lack of information leads to inappropriate processing of data.

For	Against
• cross-cultural studies – depth learned	• 'dumbells' version of Muller-Lyer
• explains many different illusion types	• cannot explain accuracy and speed of perception in novel situations
• explains perceptual set.	

Ecological model of perception (Gibson, 1950)

Optic array contains all information needed for perception (no prior knowledge).

- **direct** perception – **data-driven** processing – **bottom-up processing**
- **texture and light gradients** – information about depth and surfaces
- **optic flow** patterns – movement results in areas being systematically covered and revealed
- **affordances** – perception of object includes the possibilities it affords.

For	Against
• explains perception in good lighting conditions	• cannot explain illusions
	• cannot explain perceptual set
• attempts to explain perception in real life	• cannot explain cultural differences

Computational model of perception (Marr, 1982)

Optic array provides enough information for most perception.

- light stimulating retina organised into regions of similarity and boundaries = **raw primal sketch**
- further organisation of information (e.g. Gestalt principles) = **full primal sketch**
- add depth and distance cues = **2½ D sketch** (bottom-up process up to here)
- comparison with stored information = **3D sketch** (top-down process).

For	Against
• computer programmes can be constructed to analyse information in this way	• humans are not computers – not necessarily the same method of processing
• combines bottom-up and top-down approaches	• does not explain how bottom-up and top-down systems interact
• specific explanation of processes occurring	

Cyclic model of perception (Neisser, 1967)

- **sampling** – bottom-up processes produce representation of object (no attention required)
- **directing** – attention directed towards significant representations, stored information used to construct perceptual hypothesis (top-down) – compared with bottom-up representation
- **modifying** – if 2 representations do not match, modifications must be made until they do.

Interactionist theory "analysis by synthesis".

For	Against
• combines bottom-up and top-down	• many aspects are vague
• incorporates attentional processes	• perception is faster than this model implies

1.2 Perceptual development

Methods of study

- human **neonatal depth perception** – response to various stimuli recorded (observation or heart rate), e.g. Gibson and Walk ('60) visual cliff
- human **neonatal pattern perception** – time looking at stimuli measured, e.g. Fantz ('61) face preference, Fantz and Miranda ('75) curve preference
- human **neonatal object perception** – response recorded (observation or heart rate), e.g. Bower ('64) cubes of different sizes and distances
- **animal neonate** studies, e.g. Gibson and Walk ('60) goats and kittens on visual cliff
- **restricted environments**, e.g. Blakemore and Cooper ('70) kittens in vertical world
- **cataracts patients**, e.g. von Senden ('32)
- **distortion**, e.g. Held ('65) upside-down goggles
- **cross-cultural**, e.g. Turnbull ('61) pygmy lacking depth cues.

Many infant, animal and deprivation studies.

Pattern perception

- infants prefer faces – innate sociability (Fantz ('61))
- infants prefer curves, especially on outside of objects (Fantz and Miranda ('75))
- infants look at more complex patterns with age (Haith ('76))
- circuitry for perception present at birth, refined through experience (Banks and Ginsberg ('85)).

Infants prefer symmetrical figures.

Depth perception

- 6 months old not crawl on deep side of visual cliff (Gibson and Walk ('60)) – but not newborn
- visual cliff (Campos et al. ('70)) – heart rate of 2–5 months shows interest, 6+ months shows fear – **understanding** develops with experience
- **control** of actions important for depth perception in kittens (Held and Hein, ('63))
- 2–11 weeks flinch from looming shadows (Ball and Tronick ('71)) – but subjectivity of flinch
- very young reach for close and far objects, 5 months for near only (Field ('76)) – **experience**.

Object perception

- 4–6 months reach for solid and shadows, **learn** not to reach for shadows (Bower ('65))
- trained 2–3 months respond to correct sized cube at different distances – shows **size constancy** (Bower ('64)) – but other research contradicts
- infants prefer 3D sphere to 2D circle (Fantz ('61)).

Nature vs nurture

- infants born with some innate abilities, **refined with experience** (evidence above)

- cataracts patients can perceive objects almost immediately **but not identify**
- upside-down goggles cause internal, unconscious change in perception – **experience affects perception** (Held ('65)).

Problems with research
- infant research – responses judged **subjectively** and may be biased
- **ethics** – should infants be exposed to such environments? – animal deprivation
- **maturation** may occur – a behaviour develops later, but without experience
- research **lacks ecological validity** and may be irrelevant to real life perception.

Infants do have prior experience (even if very little).

1.3 Perceptual organisation

Organisation of incoming information allows us to make sense of it, to interpret the information.

Depth (space) perception
Position of objects in space can be determined by using monocular and binocular depth cues:

Monocular	Binocular
• **linear perspective** – parallel lines converge	• **binocular disparity** – closer = more different image on each retina
• **interposition** (superposition) – close covers far	• **retinal convergence** – muscles move eyeballs, pupils point further inwards for closer objects
• **height in plane** – nearer horizon = further	• **accommodation** – lens is thicker for closer object (controlled by ciliary body)
• **texture gradients** – further = denser	
• **colour gradients** – further = bluer	
• **shadow** – covering further object	
• **relative size** – further = smaller	
• **motion parallax** – further moves slower	

Movement perception
- **motion parallax**
- If we move, all objects appear to move, if an object is moving, others are stationary.
- **point light displays** can be accurately interpreted for posture and movement (Johansson ('75)) – perception of biological movement may be innate.

Pattern recognition
- **template matching theory** – millions of templates would be needed, problems for recognition of handwriting and rotated images, would be too slow
- **prototype theory** – typical image as template, match to best fit – still require many templates
- **feature detection** – hierarchical approach, parts of stimulus perceived then integrated to form whole, e.g. Pandemonium model (Selfridge ('59)), similar objects more difficult to distinguish (evidence from Neisser ('63)).

Perceptual constancies
- **size constancy** – depth cues used to judge distance, combined with size of retinal image = size of object – far objects have very small retinal images, 'scaled up' to compensate
- **colour constancy** – a red rose looks red in daylight, lamplight, candlelight etc. – expectations

- **shape constancy** – a door is perceived as rectangular when shut, open or ajar – expectations
- **brightness constancy** – items are perceived as the same brightness in different lighting.

Illusions
There are many different types of illusion and many different explanations for them.

Geometric illusions (e.g. Muller-Lyer, Ponzo)
- can be explained by **inappropriate size constancy scaling** (Gregory ('66))
- cross-cultural studies back this up – Segall et al. ('63)
- **problem** – the M-L illusion works as 'dumb-bells', with no depth cues
- M-L and Ponzo use **linear perspective** as depth cue, Horizontal-Vertical illusion uses **closeness to horizon**.

Fictions (e.g. Kanizsa (invisible) triangle)
- can be explained by **Gestalt** laws of organisation (see below)
- or by **experience** – white triangle is most probable hypothesis.

Mechanism illusions
- **negative after-images and waterfall effect** – habituation of cells leads to opposite experience when stimulus removed
- **pi phenomenon** – 2 alternate flashing lights perceived as one moving light.

Due to physical characteristics of visual system.

Gestalt laws of organisation
- law of **proximity** – close stimuli grouped together
- law of **similarity** – similar stimuli grouped together
- law of **closure** – prefer to perceive closed figures (ignore gaps)
- law of **continuity** – stimuli following in smooth line are grouped together
- law of **similar fate** – stimuli moving together grouped together
- law of **good Gestalt** – prefer to perceive well-rounded/symmetrical figures.

1.4 Individual, social and cultural variation in perceptual organisation

Individual differences

Some aspects of perceptual set are individual, some are cultural.
- **motivation** – Gilchrist and Nesberg ('52) food pictures perceived as brighter
- **emotion** – Worthington ('64) subliminal taboo words, dots perceived as dimmer
- **past experience** – Bruner and Goodman ('47) poorer children overestimated coin size more
- **reward and punishment** – Shafer and Murphy ('74) rewarded stimulus seen in ambiguous.

Perception is different for different individuals.

Deprivation affects perception
- Gregory and Wallace ('63) SB gains sight, cannot perceive correctly.

Cultural factors
- culture affects ability to identify individuals from racial groups (Pettigrew et al. ('58))
- cultural differences in perception of illusions, e.g. Segall et al. ('63), Turnbull ('61) – depth cues are learned, culture affects learning, **'carpentered world hypothesis'**
- **problem** – Jahoda ('66) and Gregor and McPherson ('65) no evidence for such differences.

Questions

Section 1

1. What are the main theories of perception?

2. Outline two theories of perception.

3. Provide evidence for and against Gregory's hypothesis testing theory of perception.

4. Provide evidence for and against a bottom-up theory of perception.

5. List the methods of studying perceptual development.

6. What are the problems with the various methods of studying perceptual development?

7. List the main areas of research in perceptual development and outline one study for each area.

8. List the main areas of research in perceptual organisation.

9. What are the explanations for pattern recognition and depth perception?

10. Explain perceptual constancies.

11. List the ways in which individual differences can affect perceptual organisation.

12. Describe how cultural factors can affect perceptual organisation.

2 | Attention and performance limitations

2.1 Focused (selective) attention – auditory and visual

The ability to focus attention on one task/stimulus while ignoring others.

a. Focused auditory attention

Broadbent's filter model (1958)

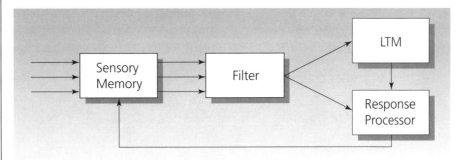

Figure 5.1

- **single channel system** – one channel attended to at a time **= serial processing**
- **limited capacity** channel – limited information carried by channel
- **early filter** – before meaning is processed
- attended channel selected by **physical characteristics** only.

For	Against
• Broadbent ('58) split span task, ear-by-ear	• Gray and Wedderburn ('60) split span task 2 channels processed together
• Cherry ('53) shadowing task, only physical characteristics of unattended noticed	• Moray ('59) name was noticed on unattended by 1/3 participants
• Moray ('59) name repeated on unattended up to 35 times – not noticed	• what is a channel? – this is not clear

Triesman's attenuation model (1964)

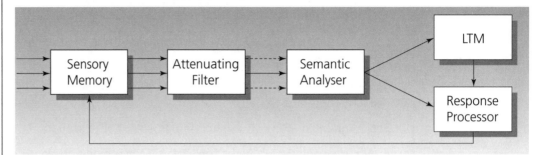

Attenuating filter –
unattended channels
are weakened, not
blocked.

Figure 5.2

- **attenuating filter** – unselected channels attenuated (weakened), not blocked
- **early filter** – selected channel chosen by physical characteristics
- **semantic analyser** – contains dictionary units (some important or particularly relevant ones have a low triggering threshold)
- usually only selected channel triggers dictionary units and reaches attention
- important information on unselected can trigger low threshold dictionary units – some unselected information is processed semantically.

For

- Moray ('59) name has low threshold dictionary unit
- explains all aspects of cocktail party phenomenon
- attenuation observed in brain regions

Against

- attenuator is not explained clearly
- 2 filters – attenuator and semantic analyser (seems inefficient)
- semantic analysis of unattended is greater than model suggests

Deutsch and Deutsch's pertinence model (1963)

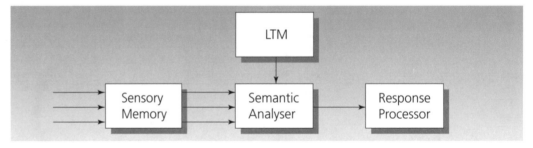

All incoming
information reaches
semantic analyser.

Figure 5.3

- **late filter** – after meaning analysed
- **all incoming information is processed semantically** at a basic level (requires stored information from LTM)
- initial semantic processing is in **parallel**, further processing is **serial**
- the **most pertinent** channel is selected and processed further and responded to.

For

- Moray ('59) name is pertinent
- Gray and Wedderburn ('60) all analysed semantically, in parallel
- Corteen and Wood ('75) semantic processing so GSR produced to synonym

Against

- inefficient use of processing power
- early work suggests meaning of unattended is not processed
- Triesman and Geffen ('67) unattended not analysed as fully

Dynamic processing model – Johnston and Heinz (1978)

- **flexible filter** – depends on incoming information
- **early filter (physical characteristics) when possible** – more efficient use of processing power
- **late filter only** when incoming information cannot be separated using physical characteristics alone – meaning must be analysed.

Flexible filter.

For

- Johnston and Heinz's ('78) targeted word study shows that the filter position is flexible

Problems with research so far

- studies are laboratory based – **lack ecological validity**
- shadowing tasks are **difficult** – may prevent analysis of unattended channel
- all investigate incoming auditory information – **cannot generalise** from this
- all models based on **Information Processing Approach**
- **ignores** ability to divide attention between tasks
- suggests brain cannot perform several processing tasks in parallel.

b. Focused visual attention

Zoom-lens model (Erikson, 1990)

- focused visual attention is like a spotlight
- within spotlight of attention stimuli are seen clearly
- spotlight can zoom in/out on smaller/larger areas.

For

- LaBerge ('83) with narrow beam of attention, fast response in central area only (wide beam fast over large area)

Against

- Juola et al. ('91) ring-shaped attention
- Neisser and Becklen ('75) attention can be targetted on specific object

Feature integration theory (Triesman, 1988)

Arisen from **visual search research** – grids of letters – time to detect presence/absence of target. Grids vary in the **features** of non-targets and targets, **number** and **position** of stimuli.

- **initial processing is rapid and parallel** – visual features of objects are processed simultaneously (no attention required)
- visual features are **combined (integrated) via serial processing** to produce objects (attention required)
- **illusory conjunctions** may be produced if not using focused attention or stored knowledge.

Initial, parallel processing is more rapid than later, serial processing.

For

- Triesman and Gelade ('80) target features (parallel) detected more rapidly than target objects (serial – integration of features)

Against

- Humphreys et al. ('85) increasing no. of non-targets did not affect detection time (if serial – should take longer with more)

Attentional engagement theory (Duncan and Humphreys, 1989)

- all visual items processed together initially – **initial parallel perceptual analysis**
- some items are selected for later processing and enter **visual STM**
- items **similar to target** also enter STM – greater similarity between target and non-target leads to longer search times
- very similar items can be **perceptually grouped** together – and then selected/rejected
- less similarity between non-targets, longer search time for target.

For

- Humphreys et al. ('85) all non-targets identical so were grouped and rejected
- Triesman and Gelade ('80) object detection slower due to similarities between target and non-targets

2.2 Divided attention

We can often carry out more than one task at once (e.g. walking and talking) **= divided attention**. This can be explained by **capacity models of attention** – we have a certain amount of attention which can be divided up between various tasks.

General capacity model (Kahneman, 1973)

- **limited capacity** of attention
- **overall capacity varies** – smaller if tired, greater if alert, smaller if terrified
- **central processor** allocates attention to different tasks
- if total demand for attention is greater than capacity, some tasks will not be attended to
- **general disposition and short-term intentions** affect which tasks are attended to.

Different tasks require different amounts of attentional capacity.

For

- explains divided and focused attention (focus when one task requires all/most attentional capacity)
- automatic tasks can be carried out simultaneously, e.g. Spelke et al. ('76)

Against

- Posner and Snyder ('75) Stroop effect – we are not free to allocate resources
- Segall and Fusella ('70) response time greater when main and secondary tasks used same processor (visual or auditory)

Specific capacity model (Allport, 1972)

- **several, independent** processors = **multichannel processor model**
- **separate** processors for **sense modalities**, each with attentional capacity
- **no central processor** for allocation of attentional resources.

Tasks only compete for attention if use same sense modality.

For

- Segall and Fusella ('70) slower response when 2 tasks use same sense modality
- Allport et al. ('72) cannot shadow and learn words, can shadow and learn pictures

Against

- does not explain why we stop talking when driving at a difficult junction
- much evidence from skilled participants – practice has made tasks automatic

Synthesis theory (Baddeley, 1986)
- combines general and specific capacity models
- **several, independent processors**
- **central processor** allocates attentional resources to specific processors.

For

- All research quoted above can be explained.

2.3 Automatic processing

Requires little attention and occurs unconsciously.

Shiffrin and Schneider (1977)
- distinguished between two main types of processing: **automatic** and **attentional** (controlled) processing:

Automatic	Attentional
can be performed in parallel	only one process can be carried out at a time (serial processing – focused attention)
require little attention and are unconscious	require attention
automatic tasks are difficult to alter	attentional tasks can be altered
tasks become automatic through practice	usually conscious
automatic tasks are unavoidable	

Evidence
- **tasks can become automatic** through practice: Hirst et al. ('80) – reading aloud and writing down dictated words simultaneously became possible with considerable practice
- the **Stroop effect** (Stroop ('35)) – reading is automatic and unavoidable.

Norman and Shallice (1980)
- two types of processing was too simplistic. When does a task stop being attentional? Suggested three levels of functioning:
  1. **Fully-automatic processing** – no attention required, unconscious, schemas organise actions
  2. **Partially-automatic processing** – some attention required from time to time to prevent disruption of behaviour
  3. **Controlled processing** – full attention required, deliberate control.

Problem: neither description explains how practice enables tasks to become automatic.

Logan (1988)
- suggested practice enables several, separate tasks to be combined into one – by combination of the separate schemas – and less processing is required.

2.4 Performance deficits

Action slips (unintended actions)
- reason ('79) divided action slips into **five categories of failure**: storage (40%); test (20%); subroutine (18%); discrimination (11%); programme assembly (5%)
- explained action slips occurring by two modes of cognitive operation:

Action slips more likely with automatic (open loop) processes.

open loop – fast, not use mental resources, inflexible, can produce action slips
closed loop – attention required, actions monitored and feedback provided, action slips unlikely.

- Sellen and Norman ('92) explained using **hierarchical schema theory**
- major schema consists of many subordinate schemas
- action slips due to **faulty triggering** of schemas by environmental cues or **faulty specification** of overall intention (so another schema is more easily activated).

Dual-task limitations

Three factors affect dual-task performance:

Task similarity – more similar tasks are more difficult to carry out simultaneously. Segall and Fusella ('70), Allport et al. ('72) – see above – are examples using the same stimulus modalities. McLeod ('77) showed that similarity of response type affects performance too.

Difficult to define how similar 2 tasks are.

Practice – Hirst et al. ('80) and Spelke et al. ('76) showed that initially impossible combinations of tasks can be performed after much practice.

Task difficulty – if one task becomes more difficult, it will affect performance of another task. Sullivan ('76) increased difficulty of shadowing task, fewer targets detected on unattended.
Duncan ('79) 2 tasks simultaneously can take more attention than the 2 tasks separately.

Questions

Test yourself – then check your answers.

Section 2

1. What are the models of auditory and visual focused attention?

2. State five important aspects of Broadbent's filter theory of focused auditory attention.

3. Provide two pieces of evidence for and against Broadbent's theory.

4. What is the main difference between the pertinence model compared to Treisman's and Broadbent's?

5. What are the problems with the research into auditory focused attention?

6. Outline the zoom-lens model of focused visual attention.

7. What are the arguments for and against the feature integration theory?

8. List the theories of divided attention.

9. Outline the general capacity model of divided attention.

10. State the arguments for and against the specific capacity model of divided attention.

11. Outline the theories of automatic processing.

12. Give evidence for and against Shiffrin and Schneider's theory of automatic processing.

13. What are the 2 explanations for action slips?

14. Which 3 factors affect dual task performance?

3 | Memory

3.1 Models of memory

3 stages of memory (processes): encoding; storage; retrieval.

1. Structure of memory

Sensory memory (sensory buffer stores, sensory input stores)
- separate stores for each modality, sensory form of stimulus is retained
- very short duration (1 sec. visual – (Sperling ('60))).

Short term memory (STM)
- **capacity** = 7+/-2 chunks (Miller ('56) – chunk can be number, letter, word etc.)
- **duration** = 30 sec. max. (Peterson and Peterson ('59) – delayed recall of trigrams)
- **coding** = acoustic (Conrad ('64) (substitution errors), Baddeley ('66)).

Long term memory (LTM)
- **capacity and duration** = unlimited
- **coding** = mainly semantic (Baddeley ('66)), some acoustic (Brown and McNeill ('66) – tip-of-the-tongue phenomenon), some visual (remembering faces etc.).

Models of memory

Multi-store model (Atkinson and Shiffrin, 1968)

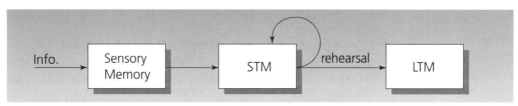

Figure 5.4

For	Against
• Glanzer and Cunitz ('66) serial position effect (primacy = LTM, recency = STM)	• Bekerian and Baddeley ('80) rehearsal is not a good transfer mechanism
• Waugh and Norman ('65) displacement occurs	• Morris ('82) passive STM not real life
• amnesics (e.g. HM) show separate stores	• amnesic HM – no LTM but learned new skills

Modifications to LTM to improve model:

Tulving ('72) **semantic** memory = general knowledge – dictionary and encyclopaedia
episodic memory = memories of events
Squire ('87) **procedural** memory = skills, schema based
declarative memory = knowledge of facts (semantic and episodic memories).

Working memory (Baddeley and Hitch, 1974)
- **modification** of STM of multi-store model
- **central executive** (CE) – limited capacity, allocates resources to other units
- **articulatory loop** (AL) – rehearsal
- **visuo-spatial scratch pad and acoustic store** – code visual and auditory information.

Structural model of memory.

Structural model of STM.

For

- Hitch and Baddeley ('76) cannot do reasoning task and recite random numbers (requires CE and AL) but can recite 1, 2, 3, 4, 5, 6 (AL only)

Against

- much evidence from lab. studies
- CE is not clearly explained

Levels of processing model (Craik and Lockhart, 1972)

- **more deeply** processed information is **retained for longer**
- **more important/**meaningful information is processed **more deeply**
- **semantic processing is deeper** than acoustic, is deeper than visual.

For

- Craik and Tulving ('75) recall best with semantic, worst with visual coding
- Hyde and Jenkins ('73) best recall with semantic processing

Against

- description rather than explanation
- semantic=LTM, visual and auditory=STM ?
- Baddeley ('78) circular depth argument
- depth of processing cannot be measured

3.2 Organisation of information in memory

Hierarchical semantic networks (Collins and Quillian, 1969)

- information organised hierarchically
- general concepts held higher up network, specific concepts lower down – more efficient
- nodes (pieces of information) are semantically linked together.

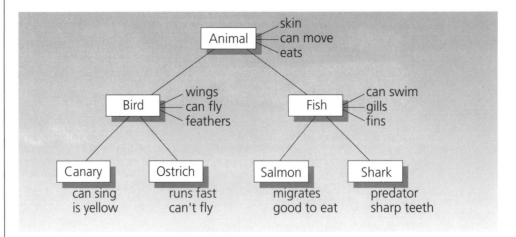

Figure 5.5 Hierarchical semantic networks

For

- Bousfield ('53) recall clustering
- Collins and Quillian ('69) sentence verification tasks
- Bower et al. ('69) categorised information has greater recall

Against

- typicality effects – typical items verified sooner
- Conrad ('72) more commonly heard phrases verified sooner

Interconnected semantic networks (Collins and Loftus, 1975)
- concepts organised in **semantic clusters**, not hierarchically
- more **similar concepts closer** together
- structure depends on **personal experience** (not scientific labels)
- **negative** links included.

Revision of hierarchical model.

Schema theory (Bartlett, 1932)
- retrieval of information often involves **reconstruction**
- reconstruction requires **prior knowledge**, uses schemas
- memory recalled is not exact reproduction of event as it occurred
- memory is an **active** process.

Memory is an active process.

For	Against
• Bartlett ('32) War of the Ghosts – transformation of information • allows for personal organisation	• over-emphasis on memory problems • influence of schemas could be at input, storage or retrieval – not clear which

3.3 Forgetting

Occurs in STM and LTM and at any of 3 stages of memory (encoding, storage, retrieval).

Encoding failure
- information was **never stored** in memory.

Trace decay
- **erosion** of memory trace by normal metabolic processes
- Gleitman ('71) more rapid trace decay in goldfish at higher temperatures
- does not explain retrieved memories (previously forgotten).

Displacement
- new information **overwrites** existing information
- applies to STM only
- **evidence** – Waugh and Norman ('65), Shallice ('67).

Different theories of forgetting explain memory loss in different situations.

Interference
- other memories **interfere** with memory being sought
- **retroactive** = new memories interfere with existing memories
- **proactive** = existing memories interfere with new memories
- more similar information, more interference (McGeogh and McDonald ('31))
- explains retrieved memories – only inaccessible, not removed.

Lack of consolidation
- **retrograde amnesia** – forget most recent events, not consolidated due to traumatic event
- evidence from ECT and concussion
- some consolidation may occur in REM sleep.

Cue- or context-dependent forgetting
- lack of correct **retrieval cues** causes forgetting
- cues entered at same time as memory (**encoding specificity principle**)
- Godden and Baddeley ('75) scuba divers recall better in same context as encoded information
- Goodwin et al. ('69) internal cues affect recall of alcoholics (**state-dependent memory**).

Motivated forgetting

- **repression** of traumatic memories – buried in unconscious mind
- neutral memories forgotten due to **association** with traumatic memories
- Levinger and Clark ('93) immediate recall of emotionally charged words is poor.

3.4 Practical applications

a. Eyewitness testimony

- memories are often **partially reconstructed** – not exact copies of events = **confabulation**
- **confabulation/reconstruction** uses existing schemas
- **leading questions** elicit different answers from non-leading (Loftus and Zanni ('75))
- **hypnotism** increases confabulation – highly motivated to please
- Orne ('51) hypnotised witness identified suspect who was out of the country!
- eyewitness accounts are **unreliable** – but juries are not necessarily aware of this.

Witnesses tell their own version of the events.

b. Memory for medical information

- patients often have **poor recall** of medical information
- this can be damaging for patient, or lead to slow recovery, or lead to complaints
- Ley ('78) used research findings to produce guidelines for doctors
  repeat important information – or ask the patient to repeat
  simplify information – short words and phrases
  give **specific** advice and important information first (**primacy effect**)
  organise information in sub-sections, e.g. medication, appointments
  send **reminders** (written or telephone)
- these guidelines improved patients' memory for medical information (55% to 70%).

Mnemonic techniques (improvement of memory)

- **rehearse** information to transfer it to LTM
- **organise** information into categories – improves recall (e.g. Bower et al. ('69))
- use **acronyms**, e.g. ROY G. BIV, or other abbreviations – provides meaning
- use **visual imagery** – helps to form links and organise information
- use **keywords** – for foreign languages, uses visual imagery
- **method of loci** – for memorising lists, uses visual imagery
- **peg words** – new words linked to existing peg words (1- bun, 2- shoe, etc.).

Use these to help with revision.

Questions

Section 3

1. What are the three processes of memory?

2. What are the three separate memory structures often referred to?

3. List the main models of memory.

4. List the main aspects of the multi-store model.

5. State evidence for and against the levels of processing model.

6. List the three theories of organisation of information in memory.

7. Outline the hierarchical semantic networks explanation.

8. Give evidence for and against the schema theory.

9. List the theories of forgetting.

10. Provide evidence for three theories of forgetting.

11. List the main practical applications of memory research.

12. Outline the implications of memory research for eyewitness testimony.

Test yourself – then check your answers.

4 | Language and thought

4.1 Language acquisition

Learning theory (Skinner, 1957)
- language learned gradually by **operant conditioning**
- initial babbling (random noises) – **selective reinforcement** narrows range of sounds
- sounds eventually form words via **behaviour shaping** process (successive approximations)
- words put together into phrases – reinforcement continues to shape behaviour.

Nature – nurture debate over language acquisition.

For	Against
• explains learning of sounds and simple meanings	• Brown et al. ('69) mothers reinforce meaning not correct grammar
• Engel et al. ('75) develop faster if listen to more speech	• only considers performance (use) not competence (understanding)
• Olsen et al. ('86) use of responsive language speeds development	• spontaneous use of rules (e.g. plurals)
• Motherese helps language development (Gelman and Shatz ('77))	• universal sequence of stages of development
	• novel utterances – creativity of language

Nativist theory (Chomsky, 1959)
- language acquisition **too rapid** to be explained by operant conditioning
- **innate mechanism** for language development – language acquisition device (**LAD**)
- language has **deep** (meaning) and **surface** (actual words used) structure
- **transformational grammar** used to extract deep from surface structure.

Are humans unique in use of language?

For	Against
• explains universal sequence of language development – maturation process	• ignores learning – children in isolation do not develop language (e.g. Genie)
• explains overgeneralisations	• Akiyama ('84) languages not as similar as Chomsky thought
• language areas of brain not found in other animals	

Interactionist theories

Cognitive (Piaget)
- **maturation** and **experience** important
- **cognitive changes** allow development of language
- child is **active learner** – tests rules of language (similar to other areas of development).

For	Against
• rapid increase in vocabulary at 18 months – indicates maturation?	• no correlation between object permanence and language development once age factor removed (Corrigan ('78))
• relational words (more, up) may depend on object permanence	

Social-interactionist
- biological and cognitive processes are not enough to explain language development
- **communication** is main function of language
- **LASS** (language acquisition socialisation system) – early social interaction
- language reflects culture.

For	Against
• can be used to extend other theories	• deprived children show impaired language

4.2 Production and comprehension of speech

Production – speech and writing

Speech
- **planning** before speech – **hesitation-analysis** studies, e.g. Goldman-Eisler ('68) longer pauses when less predictable content to follow
- **phoneme** errors (incorrect letter): exchange; anticipation; perseveration; deletion
- **morpheme** errors (incorrect meaning unit): exchange; deletion
- **word** errors: exchange; blend; substitution
- Brown and McNeill ('68) **tip-of-the-tongue** phenomenon – 57% recall first letter correctly
- Harley ('95) know meaning of what we want to say, but not retrieve sound.

- **Garrett** ('88) **model of speech production** – five independent levels of processing, one after another – serial process: **message** (concept formed); **functional** (grammar planning); **positional** (word order); **sound** (pronunciation); **articulatory** (articulation instructions).

- **Spreading activation theory** (Dell ('86)) – four processing stages, all work concurrently – parallel process, higher levels slightly ahead of lower, activation spreads through network via a lexicon (dictionary): **semantic** (meaning); **syntactic** (grammar); **morphological** (units of meaning); **phonological** (units of sound).

Evaluation of models
Harley ('95) argues some parallel processing occurs
Anticipation errors suggest some **serial** processing.
Spreading activation accounts for **feedback** (correction of errors by speaker in mid-sentence).

Writing
- many cognitive components **shared** with speech production
- less likely to exhibit **hesitations** and **errors** of speech
- Hayes and Flower ('86) three stages in process: **planning**; **sentence generation**; **reviewing**
- **sentence generation** – partial sentences developed, then final chosen (Kaufer et al. ('86))
- **reviewing** – expert better than novice, spend longer, assess whole text not just sentences
- **spelling** – known words in **grapheme output lexicon**, unknown built via **phoneme–grapheme conversion** (phoneme = sound, grapheme = letters representing sound).

Comprehension – listening and reading

Listening
- **identification and interpretation** of speech sounds – several difficulties:
  - i. **word boundaries** are not clear
  - ii. **phonemes** run into one another

Much work on speech errors.

2 theories of speech production.

Both explain many speech error findings.

Writing is more formal and accurate than speech.

iii. surrounding **noise** must be filtered out and any gaps filled in
iv. **phoneme differentiation** – this is a learned ability.
- **visual information** aids listening – Massaro ('89) lip reading = bottom-up methods
- top-down method – Warren and Warren ('70) **phonemic restoration effect**
- Liberman et al. ('67) **motor theory** of speech perception – production of sounds uses motor skills and aids comprehension – but infants can recognise some before they speak
- Marslen-Wilson ('90) **cohort model** – integrates bottom-up and top-down processes –
  i. **B-U**: all words like stimulus heard are targeted – **word-initial cohort**
  ii. **T-D**: meaning of surrounding words eliminates words from i.
- Marslen-Wilson and Tyler ('80) targets identified more rapidly if context had meaning (T-D).

Reading

- reading must be **learned** – match shapes to sounds
- **maturation** – Gibson et al. ('62) distinctive features of letter shapes less recognisable to pre-school children
- amount taken in per fixation = **perceptual span** (good readers have large p.s.)
- 3 main types of explanation (B-U):
  i. **direct-access** – visual information is enough to recognise words
  ii. **indirect-access** – words translated into sounds which are then analysed
  iii. **dual-encoding** – both i. and ii. can access meanings.
- T-D processes important (in experienced readers) – Carpenter and Dahneman ('81) more time spent on unexpected words.

4.3 Models of thought

Problem-solving

- problems are very diverse, therefore there may not be a single framework for solving them
- **people use heuristic thought** (selective) to solve problems whereas **computers use algorithmic thought** and go through all possible combinations/permutations
- **Information Processing Approach** (IPA) important – Newell et al. ('58) 3 stages: representation; selection and implementation; evaluation (allows feedback).

Means-ends analysis (Newells and Simon, 1963)

- **problem-space** theory (p.s. is distance between current position and goal state (solution))
- **sub-goal** created, select operator to reach sub-goal (problem now partially solved)
- **assess** distance to goal, **create new sub-goal**, closer to ultimate goal etc.

Analogy approach

- use **earlier solution** to help with new problem
- not always easy to notice analogy, so not use it
- Novick and Holyoak ('91) analogy approach requires four processes: **locate** source problem (analogy); **compare** source and target problem; **adapt** useful procedures from source problem; **develop** schema for whole class of problems
- experts use analogy approach more than novices (Novick ('88)).

Factors influencing problem-solving

- **mental set** – 'set up' to respond in particular way – Luchins ('42) use same method even when not appropriate
- **expertise** – experts better at problem solving than novices
- **problem definition** – original and goal state are not always clear in real life = ill-defined, may not be one single solution, difficult to tell if solution correct
- **functional fixedness** – Duncker ('45) once object used in one way, this function is fixed.

Top-down or bottom-up?

Reading must be learned – match shapes to sounds.

2 main models.

Heuristic approach.

Reasoning

Making logical inferences from information presented.

- **deductive** reasoning = making **specific inferences** from a general rule
- **inductive** reasoning = specific cases are used to **generate a general rule**
- two types of deductive reasoning: **propositional** and **categorical**
- **propositional** – if... then... statements – valid and invalid conclusions:
  valid = affirming antecedent; denying consequent
  invalid = denying antecedent; affirming consequent
  Taplin ('71) invalid type statements more difficult to interpret
  many possible reasons – illicit conversion, mental models, confirmation and matching bias
- **categorical** – syllogisms = argument with 2 premises (statements), 1 conclusion
  participants asked to judge validity of conclusion, e.g. Wason selection task ('66)
  more difficult if negatives or passive voice (Lippman ('72))
  Markovits and Nantel ('89) belief-bias affects reasoning – judge using knowledge not premises
- these types of reasoning are rare in real life situations.

4.4 Theories and evidence linking language and thought

Range of views on relationships between language and thought.

Extreme view.

much argument over the relationship between language and thought
most extreme views = language is essential for thought, thought does not require language

Sapir-Whorf hypothesis
- language determines thought – limited language, limited thought – Sapir ('58), Whorf ('56)
- Carroll and Casangrande ('58) Navaho language stresses form, Navaho children better at recognition of form
- alternative interpretation possible – experience affects recognition ability.

Linguistic relativity hypothesis
- language affects thought
- wider vocabulary allows more cognitive discrimination
- much evidence from differing vocabularies in different languages
- Eskimo snow words wildly exaggerated, no more than in English (12) (Pinker ('94))
- alternative explanation – need to discriminate generates new vocabulary.

Language affects some cognitive processes
- specific processes can be affected by language used
- Loftus et al. ('78) leading questions produce different responses to non-leading
- Carmichael et al. ('32) labels can affect perception and memory of drawings
- Bernstein ('61) restricted code language does not allow conceptualisation of abstract concepts.

Some thought is independent of language
- some innate capacity for discrimination
- colour perception does not require language
- Furth ('66) deaf people carry out thought processes.

Piaget's developmental approach
- cognitive development is required for linguistic development
- language is one type of symbolic function
- Sinclair-de-Zwart ('69) non-conservers do not use relative terms (e.g. bigger).

Vygotsky's developmental approach
- language and thought develop independently initially
- language develops for communication in social situations (pre-intellectual language)

- basic thinking skills develop independently (pre-linguistic thought)
- 2 merge at about 2 yrs old, language now shapes thought, which becomes more complex.

4.5 Social and cultural variations

- different societies and cultures have different languages, or use of language
- if language affects thought, then society/culture will have an effect on thought via language
- evidence for the effect of language on thought is ambiguous (see Section 4.4 above)
- some vocabulary differences do exist between different languages, e.g. Dani have only black and white to denote colour (Rosch ('78)), Arabs have several words for sand
- evidence for different cultures having different vocabularies has often been exaggerated
- elaborate vs restricted code forms of language – lower SES tend to use restricted code only – limits conceptualisation of abstract concepts – SES affects thought (Bernstein ('73))
- non-standard language forms have also been studied, e.g. 'black English' – dialect spoken in some black communities
- Labov ('70) standard and non-standard forms allow same concepts to be expressed, but – non-standard speaker will be disadvantaged in situation where standard is used.

Section 4

1. List the main theories of language acquisition.

2. Explain how learning theory accounts for language acquisition.

3. State arguments for and against learning theory as an explanation of language acquisition.

4. Outline the nativist theory of language acquisition.

5. Outline the two models of speech production.

6. Assess the plausibility of the models of speech production.

7. List the main factors in the production of writing.

8. What are the main explanations of speech comprehension (listening)?

9. What are the main explanations of reading?

10. Assess the importance of top-down and bottom-up processes in reading and writing.

11. Outline the approaches to problem-solving.

12. What are the different types of reasoning?

13. Provide evidence for language affecting thought.

14. Provide evidence for thought affecting language.

15. Briefly outline the explanations for the relationship between language and thought.

16. Do different cultures have different vocabularies, and would this affect thought?

17. What are elaborate and restricted code forms of language, and their effects on thought?

Chapter six

Developmental psychology

1 | Early socialisation

1.1 Early social development

a. Sociability

- tendency of infant to want to interact with others
- **nature-nurture** debate over whether sociability is innate or learned
- several approaches to explain development of sociability.

Learning theory and social learning theory
- **reinforcement** builds up stimulus-response links
- social learning theory includes **imitation** and **observation**
- **speech** is inadequately explained
- order of **behaviour acquisition** is not explained.

Piaget
- **cognitive development** required for social interactions to take place
- social interactions same as any other interactions with environment.

Vygotsky
- **social interaction essential** for other development
- understanding first occurs in social environment.

Innate capacities
- infants respond to people differently from other objects they encounter (**innate response**)
- **turn-taking** occurs in 'conversations' between parent and infant – innate (Trevarthen ('69))
- infants show specific movements, e.g. **pre-speech mouth movements** when interacting with adults.

Neonatal capabilities

Imitation
- important for development of social skills (Stern ('77))
- neonates will imitate several behaviours: lip-pursing; mouth opening; finger movements
- neonatal imitation stops by 7 wks, reappears at 7–12 mths
- older children imitate sounds as well as visual signals.

Perceiving faces
- Fantz ('61) babies prefer to look at faces than other shapes – **innate sociability**?
- 12 hr old will prefer to look at mother than stranger
- focal length set at about 21cm (approx. distance to mother's face when held in arms).

Smiling
- Freedman ('74) half-smiles at few days old (not wind!), social smiles about 6 wks
- **innate response** – cross-cultural evidence, blind children smile to voices at same age
- may be a **survival strategy** – rewards mother, increased likelihood of continued care.

Contingency
- Watson & Ramey ('72) particularly responsive to events dependent on own actions
- infant has **control** over environment, and **consequences** of actions.

Transactions
- exchanges of behaviour important for **social development**
- babies and parents follow each other's movements = **interactional synchronicity**
- respond best to 'Motherese'
- turn-taking behaviour may be important for language development (Snow ('79)).

Crying
- Wolff ('69) identified at least 3 types of cry: hunger; pain; anger
- mothers can tell the difference between cries.

b. Attachment

- an affectional bond to a specific person – the **attachment figure**
- Maccoby ('80) a relatively enduring emotional tie to a specific person
- attachment is from infant to figure, but **mutual interaction** is important.

Function
- **security** – safe base to explore from
- **first relationship** = basis for later ones
- to learn about later social relationships – learns from attachment figure
- Rutter ('81) aim = detachment (eventually).

Identifying attachments
Attachment can be assumed if attachment behaviours are shown:
- **seeking** attachment figure (AF) when anxious, AF reduces anxiety
- AF used as **safe base** for exploration
- **stranger fear/anxiety** = from 6 mths to 2 yrs, reduced if AF present
- **separation anxiety** = distress at separation from AF, peaks at 14–18 mth, over by 3 yrs – pattern of behaviours observed: distress; despair; detachment
- both anxieties are cross-cultural & not highly affected by rearing techniques
- possible explanation – increased memory and object permanence at 6 mth.

Development of attachments
- Schaffer ('77) three stages: 1 – **attach** to any human; 2 – **can distinguish** but accepts care from anyone; 3 – **bonds with specific** AF
- Bowlby ('69) (see theory below) 5 stages:
  1 – **sociable to all**; 2 – **sociable to few** (5 mth); 3 – tries to be **close to AF** (5–7 mth); 4 – **partnership** with AF, cares for them, sees their point of view (3 yr); 5 – maintain relationship when **separated** (e.g. at school) (5 yr)
- Bee ('91) infant shows attachment behaviour to **attract** AF, then **bonds**, AF's bond to infant is **strengthened** by attachment behaviour.

Factors affecting attachment
- Schaffer and Emerson ('64) more likely to attach to those sensitive to and responding to needs = **sensitive responsiveness**
- irritability of infant at 5–10 days linked with **attachment type** (irritable – insecure)
- **skin-to-skin** contact may be important for mother's bond to child (Klaus and Kennell ('76)).

Types of attachment
- **strength** = how intensely attachment behaviours exhibited
- **security** = confidence in relationship, ease of use of AF as safe base
- Ainsworth et al. ('78) 'strange situation', 3 types of attachment found:
  anxious-avoidant (15%); **securely attached** (70%); **anxious-resistant** (15%)
- **secure attachments** associated with **sensitive responsiveness** in parent.

Characteristics associated with attachment.

Attachment changes over time.

Sensitive parents tend to have secure babies.

Theories of attachment

Behaviourist
- **Learning Theory** – classical conditioning
- **food = primary reinforcer**, associated with mother (secondary reinforcer)
- **cupboard love** – cannot explain attachments to non-caregivers.

Psychodynamic theory
- mother **satisfies needs** of infant so infant wants to be near her
- **food = primary drive**, mother = secondary drive
- **cupboard love** – cannot explain attachments to non-caregivers.

Bowlby
- lack of attachment = **maternal deprivation**
- critical period for attachment = up to 2 yrs, no bond by then leads to **affectionless psychopathy**
- evidence for affectionless psychopathy from juvenile delinquents (maternal separations)
- relationship with AF is qualitatively different to others = **monotropy**.

Problems
- deprivation not the same as privation (see below)
- Rutter et al. ('76) separation not always lead to delinquency
- quality more important than quantity for attachment.

1.2 Enrichment and deprivation

Enrichment

- **Head Start** – US enrichment programme – initial IQ increases – small and did not last
- Lazar and Darlington ('82) follow-up project, less likely to leave school early, be delinquent
- **Milwaukee Project** – Heber et al. ('72) helped infants and mothers (low social class, Black, low IQ), IQ gains for children of 10 points (average)
- **High/Scope** – Berreuta-Clement et al. ('84) US field expt, significant differences in later life compared to controls: fewer yrs special education, more employment and graduation
- Skeels and Dye ('39) extra stimulation benefits cognitive and language development
- Furman et al. ('79) social development can be enhanced by peer-therapy.

Deprivation = loss of attachment

Short-term separation
- a number of factors affect the response to short-term separation: **age**; **gender**; **experience**; **boredom**; **quality of substitute care**.

Childminding and working parents
- Kagan et al. ('80) no difference between daycare and homecare children
- Rubenstein and Howes ('79) may be long-term benefits to peer interactions.

Hospitalisation
- Spitz and Wolf ('46) if >3 mth separation, made full recovery from anaclitic depression
- Douglas ('75) separation of >1wk for child <4yrs associated with behaviour disturbance.

Long-term separation

Divorce
- Richards ('87) divorce more serious consequences than death of father (children resent parents, parents give biased views, sooner remarriage more likely = stressful)
- Cockett and Tripp ('94) more health problems, low self-esteem, friendship troubles.

Death
- depression more likely than delinquency

Why do attachments develop?

Maternal care as important as food and physical care.

Quality and stability of substitute care = most important.

- critical period – high rate of depression only in over 6 yrs (Bifulco et al. ('92)).

Adoption
- Hodges and Tizard ('89) children in adopted families no different to normal at 16 yrs
- Triseliotis ('80) long-term foster care in single home leads to normal development.

c. Privation

= total lack of attachment, rather than loss of one (deprivation).

Institution care
- Skeels and Dye ('39) IQ increased after transfer to more stimulating environment
- Goldfarb ('43) institution children showed less development than fostered
- Bowlby ('46) affectionless psychopathy in juvenile delinquents (but retrospective study)
- Bowlby ('56) little difference between long-term hospitalisation group and normal.

Case studies of isolated children
- **Czech. twins** (Koluchova ('76)) – found at 7 yrs – initially terrified, by 14 yrs seemed normal, still fine at 20 yrs, above average IQ (attachment to each other important?)
- **Genie** (Curtiss ('77)) – found 12 yrs – developed only a little language
- **Children of the Holocaust** (Freud and Dann ('51)) at 3 yrs had strong attachments to each other, later lives relatively normal (some form of attachment important?)
- **Isabelle** (Davis ('47)) – found 6 yrs – could not speak – quick recovery
- **problems** – small samples; could be due to genetic problems rather than privation.

1.3 Variation in childrearing

Cultural variation
- Sidell ('72) Israeli kibbutz, infants cared for mainly by nursery staff, still attached to mother, **multiple attachments**
- Ainsworth ('67) Ugandan tribe (Ganda) **multiple attachments** = normal, and earlier
- Kagan and Klein ('75) isolated Guatemalan region, >1 yr unstimulated, **no later ill-effects**
- Ochs and Schieffelin ('84) Samoans and Kaluli children gain speech without Motherese or conversational speech from mother when very young.

Social variation
- Newson and Newson ('68) working class parents encourage children to stand up for themselves, not so for middle class
- Jones ('87) less breastfeeding in lower SES families – has effect on health and intelligence
- **society changes over time** – so have breast-feeding practices – now 'on demand'.

Summary
- research shows that there are a **variety of styles** of child-rearing practices
- it is not only Western practices that produce healthy, stable, intelligent children
- **cross-cultural studies** show some similarities and some differences
- child-rearing practice is only **one of many variables** that could cause differences.

Section 1

1. What is sociability?

2. List the approaches attempting to explain the development of sociability.

3. List the capabilities of neonates to interact socially.

4. What are the characteristics of an attachment and how does it develop?

5. List factors affecting attachments.

Institutional care and case studies.

Several cases of severe deprivation.

Questions

6. Outline the theories of attachment.

7. What are the effects of enrichment on development?

8. What are the effects of short and long-term separation from the attachment figure?

9. What are the effects of privation?

10. What are the problems with the research into privation?

11. List cultural variations in childrearing practices and any differences in development associated with them.

12. How can social variation affect child-rearing and development?

2 | Cognitive development

2.1 Theories of cognitive development

Piaget's theory of cognitive development

- **biological development** of brain directly affects (and limits) cognitive development
- schemas affected by **experience** – action important – active learning
- **assimilation** and **accommodation** of schemas are important
- accommodation returns state to equilibrium after disequilibrium
- four stage theory – stages in sequence, but ages are generalisations – evidence from cross-cultural studies, e.g. Nyiti ('76), Kiminyo ('77).

Sensorimotor (0–2yr)
direct actions and **sensory information** used to understand world
body-schema develops – me vs not-me – reduces egocentrism
object permanence develops – gradual process – reduces egocentrism
start to develop **GSF** (general symbolic function) – important for language.

Pre-operational (2–7yr)
egocentrism – egocentric illusion (3 mountains)
conservation problems – difficult due to centration – number, substance, weight, volume
preconceptual (2–4) and **intuitive** (4–7) sub-stages
preconceptual – problems with relativity, seriation, syncretic thought, animism
intuitive – classification/class inclusion tests difficult (beads or white beads?).

Concrete operational (7–11yr)
three parts to operations: **compensation**; **reversibility**; **identity**
concrete operations require presence of concrete objects
conservation and classification tasks now possible
problems with mental operations such as relativity.

Formal operational (11–15+yr)
logical problem solving (beaker problem)
concrete objects not needed for manipulation – ideas can be used – **abstract concepts**.

General criticisms of theory
- **stages** – not very useful, **decalage** occurs and development is gradual – **arbitrary** divisions – Meadows ('88) **inconsistencies** within stage
- **ages at stages** – other research differs, e.g. Bower ('81) object permanence, Rose and Blank ('74) conservation, Dasen ('77) formal operational may not always be reached (cultural)
- **development through stages can be speeded up** (e.g. Brainerd ('83), Meadows ('88))

- **methodology** – flexible interviewing techniques – non-standardised
- **task difficulty** – produced lower ages because methods too obscure:
  object permanence – Bower and Wishart ('72) infants reach if light off
  conservation – accidental (McGarrigle and Donaldson ('74) Naughty teddy) and
      incidental (Light et al. ('79) pasta race) techniques
  egocentrism – Hughes ('75) 3 mountains task vs relevant setting (policeman).

Many criticisms affect details of theory, rather than discrediting the whole theory.

Vygotsky's theory of cognitive development

- **cognitive and language development interlinked** from about 2 years old
- **active learning** but social interaction is crucial (unlike Piaget)
- **zone of proximal development** – what can do with help today, can do unaided tomorrow
- **retrospective** (already achieved) and **prospective** (could achieve) intelligence
- adults, peers and teachers important in **guiding potential development**
- four stages of concept formation (identified from own research):
  vague syncretic; **complexes**; **potential concept**; **mature concept stage**
- children learn better if aided by experts first – Freund ('90) furniture sorting with mothers.

Language and culture play major roles in cognitive development.

Bruner's theory of cognitive development

- **interaction** with environment is necessary to develop ways of representing it
- three modes of representing the world – develop in order though first not lost
  enactive mode (0–1 yrs); **iconic** mode (1–7 yrs); **symbolic** mode (7+ yrs)
- Bruner and Kenney ('66) most 6 yr olds do reproduction task (iconic) but not transposition task (symbolic) with grid of plastic glasses.

Thought dependent on language.

Information Processing Approach

- **more efficient** processing of information with age
- IPA has number of assumptions:
  1. children have **limited ability** to process information, e.g. smaller digit recall in STM
  2. children have **little experience**
  3. children **poor at using strategies** to improve performance.
- if children have experience, can perform better than adults, e.g. Chi ('78) chess
- problem for 3. – Children do use limited strategies to aid memory
- **Case's theory** – cognitive development due to more efficient strategies leading to increased information processing ability.

M space – mental space – increases with age
Practice leads to automatic processing, less M space required.

Improved efficiency with experience – development continues throughout life.

2.2 Practical applications in education

Piaget's theory

Readiness
- no point trying to teach a concept before child has cognitive capacity to understand it
- but – many of Piaget's ages are over-estimated and development can be speeded up.

Active (self-discovery) learning
- active, not passive/tutorial, learning is advocated – **development of schemas**
- **problem** – tutorial training can be as/more effective (Brainerd ('83)).

Child-centred learning techniques
- **individual learning programs** for each child (Smith and Cowie ('88))
- assess cognitive development and set appropriate, intrinsically motivating tasks

When to teach what?

- create disequilibrium so child can pass into next stage via accommodation and new schemas
- **problem** – not entirely practical in large classes.

Main changes in primary sector where active learning is used (recommended by Plowden report ('67)) – in secondary teaching, Nuffield Science syllabus emphasises self-discovery.

Vygotsky's and Bruner's theories

Scaffolding
- **expert provides support** for child – aids development through zone of proximal development
- **effective intervention**: increase help if failing, decrease if succeeding (Wood et al. ('78))
- **peer group teaching** – differences of opinion linked with most learning (Howe et al. ('91))
- Blaye et al. ('91) pairs more successful than individuals on computer problem-solving.

Information Processing Approach

- **identify good strategies** for a task and how they develop
- consistent errors indicate faulty rule being used – **try to identify it**
- **encourage meta-cognition** – thinking about why strategies work
- Brown and Burton ('78) devised computer program to train teachers to identify bugs.

2.3 Development of measured intelligence

Generally, intelligence is an ability to gather and use information in a reasoned way, resulting in effective interaction with the environment.

There are three main factors affecting measured intelligence: **genetics**; **environment**; **test bias**. There has been a nature/nurture debate which now concentrates on which has the greater effect on IQ – genes or environment.

Genetics

Twin studies
- monozygotic (identical) twins have identical genes, dizygotic (fraternal) twins do not
- Bouchard and McGue ('81) identical twins have more similar IQs (.85 correlation)
- also, identical reared apart correlation is higher than fraternal reared together
- identical twins reared together are more similar than reared apart – Shields ('62)
- studies indicate 50–80% of IQ score is due to genetic effects.

Problems
- twin studies have **small sample sizes**
- **should not assume cause and effect** relationship from correlations
- twins often separated after 1yr old – **early development** together could lead to similarities
- some adoption agencies **match adoptive families** with natural parents and environments.

Family studies
- comparison of genetic similarity and IQ score
- Bouchard and McGue ('81) found IQ correlation greater if more closely related
- **problem** – closely related tend to experience similar environment.

Adoption studies
- comparison of child's IQ with biological and adoptive parents
- **Texas Adoption Study** – Horn ('83) correlation with biological mother (.28) higher than with adoptive (.15) when aged 8 yrs

Independent learning systems.

Do not overload STM – small amounts at a time.

Intelligence is difficult to define and measure.

Should not assume cause and effect from correlations.

- Skodak and Skeels ('49) correlation with biological aged 4 (.28) lower than when 13 yrs (.44) – initial environmental effects lessen with time.

Environment

Adoption studies

- children from low socio-economic status families adopted by high SES families show increase in IQ compared to unadopted siblings – Schiff et al. ('78) environment important
- adopted children have higher IQs (10–20 points) than biological parents – adoptive parents tend to be wealthy and have higher IQs.

Intelligence may be the result of environmental factors.

Social factors

- Sameroff and Seifer ('83) 10 environmental factors influencing IQ score, e.g. mother did not go to High School, mother has serious anxiety, from minority group, father not with family, 4+ children in family
- Bernstein ('61) children in low SES families learn restricted language code – does not allow for discussion of complex, abstract concepts – environment limits
- HOME scores correlate well (.50) with later IQ scores (Caldwell and Bradley ('78))
- Caldwell and Bradley ('84) factors linked with high IQ: parents talk to child; provide appropriate play materials; are emotionally responsive; have high expectations
- Yeates et al. ('79) aged 2 yrs best IQ predictor is mother's IQ (genetic), by 4 yrs best predictor is HOME score (environment).

Test bias

IQ tests themselves account for some differences in IQ scores.

Cultural bias

- different cultures have different criteria for success – tests will reflect this
- Luria ('71) different cultures chose different odd-one-out
- Cole et al. ('71) categories for sorting items vary depending on culture
- Williams ('72) BITCH designed for black American children – white children do less well
- **care needed interpreting IQ scores** – may be result of cultural differences.

May test culturally specific knowledge.

Motivation

- Zigler et al. ('73) IQ scores improved if short play session with tester first.

Test familiarity

- familiarity with similar materials related to higher test scores (Dirks ('82))
- lack of familiarity with short answers may disadvantage black American children in IQ tests.

Questions

Section 2

1. List the main theories of cognitive development.

2. What are the key points in Piaget's theory of cognitive development?

3. Give four pieces of evidence for and against Piaget's theory.

4. Outline one other theory of cognitive development.

5. List the practical applications that have arisen from Piaget's theory.

6. List practical applications that have arisen from other theories.

7. What are the problems for these practical applications?

8. State evidence for a genetic aspect to intelligence, and evaluate this evidence.

9. State evidence for an environmental effect on intelligence.

10. How can tests themselves affect measured intelligence?

Test yourself – then check your answers.

3 | Social behaviour and diversity in development

3.1 Theories of moral development

Freud's psychodynamic theory

- **Oedipus complex** occurs during phallic stage of development (3–5/6 yrs)
- **desire for opposite-sex parent** results in same-sex parent being seen as a rival
- **fear of punishment leads to identification** with same-sex parent
- identification **resolves** Oedipus complex, produces **superego**
- **superego = conscience and ego-ideal**
- **predicts inverse relationship between guilt and wrongdoing** – more guilt, fewer wrongs
- predicts **fixed moral values** dependent on the strength of conscience.

For	Against
• MacKinnon ('38) cheats felt less guilty	• Hartshorne and May ('28) character education enquiry, inconsistent moral behaviour
	• no evidence for stronger conscience in males

Cognitive-developmental theories

stress **developmental aspect** – changes over time
stages of moral development – dependent on cognitive development
universality of moral principles

Piaget's theory of moral development

- investigated **understanding of rules**, their **moral judgements** and means of **punishment**
- moral judgements investigated using moral stories – judge by intent or consequences?
- >5 yrs children are pre-moral, do not understand rules or evaluate actions effectively
- 5-9 yrs show moral realism and heteronomous morality – follow rules of others, cannot be changed – judge moral stories by consequences (damage done) – punishment by atonement
- 9+ yrs show autonomous morality – rules can be changed by mutual consent – judge by intentions – punishment fits crime (reciprocity).

For	Against
• Piaget's ('32) work showed results above	• Armsby ('61) varied damage done, younger could judge by intention but damage affects judgement
• Linaza ('84) similar rules results in Spain	• stories confound damage and intent
• Ferguson and Rule ('82) more similar evidence, but only in Western cultures	• cross-cultural studies more ambiguous

Kohlberg's theory of moral development

- investigated **moral reasoning** using **moral dilemmas** (e.g. Heinz and druggist)
- extended moral development into adulthood
- underlying cognitive structure affects moral development more than child-rearing technique
- 3 levels of moral development, 6 stages in total (2 per level).

Level 1 – **Preconventional morality** (> about 10 yrs)	**Stage 1**: **Punishment and obedience** orientation moral action to avoid punishment **Stage 2**: **Instrumental-relativist** orientation right = fair and judged by rewards
Level 2 – **Conventional morality** (most adolescents and adults)	**Stage 3**: **Interpersonal concordance** orient. right = approved by majority, conformity **Stage 4**: **Law and order** orientation right = duty, common good of society
Level 3 – **Postconventional morality** (only 10–15% adults)	**Stage 5**: **Social contract-legalistic** orientation laws can be changed democratically **Stage 6**: **Universal-ethical principle** orient. right = own moral views and ethical principles

For

- Kohlberg ('57) longitudinal study, P's never went backwards through stages
- Kohlberg ('63) individuals have dominant stage of morality for moral dilemmas
- cross-cultural evidence – Snarey ('85)
- allows for individuals to behave differently depending on the situation – reasoning more important than actions

Against

- stages 5 and 6 are not reached by most adults – ideals rather than normal stages
- bias towards older people, most stages not relevant to children
- universal principles may not be – bias towards Western values
- biased towards male values (justice) – women's values tend towards care

Learning Theory

Moral behaviour learned by classical and operant conditioning (Chapter 2, Section 4.1).

Classical conditioning
- **conscience is several conditioned emotional responses** (CERs)
- CERs arise due to association of wrongdoing with anxiety (from being disciplined)
- eventually, thought of wrongdoing produces anxiety – don't do it!
- anxiety CER occurs before wrongdoing, guilt CER occurs after wrongdoing.

Operant conditioning
- **child controls actions, repetition likely if reinforced, less likely if punished** (Chapter 2, Section 4.1)
- rewards more effective than punishment (only suppresses behaviour)
- warm relationship between child and rewarder/punisher improves learning (Parke ('69)).

Classical and operant conditioning.

For

- Solomon et al. ('68) punished puppies before and after wrongdoing, anxiety group resist temptation for longer but less guilty
- Aronfeed ('63) similar with children

Against

- cognitive factors affect children's behaviour – e.g. reason given (Parke ('74))
- punishment can increase behaviour
- limited approach – ignores motivation

Social Learning Theory

- emphasises **observation**, **imitation** and **cognitive factors** – vicarious learning can occur

Based on Learning Theory.

Moral behaviour
may be situation –
specific.

- children imitate models who are rewarded, are similar to child, are nurturant, powerful, consistent, show appropriate behaviours, have relevance to child
- **learning occurs without reward**
  Mischel ('73) five person variables – cognitive – affect S-R: **competencies**; **cognitive strategies**; **expectancies**; **subjective outcome variables**; **self-regulatory systems and plans**.

For	Against
• Bandura ('65) children most likely to imitate attack on Bobo doll if adult rewarded, least likely if punished	• Brofenbrenner ('73) limited social situation in Bobo doll studies – no interaction
• allows for individual differences	• cognitive aspects less important than S-R links

3.2 Theories of the development of gender

Terminology
- **sex** = biological sexual status, physically male or female
- **gender/gender identity** = classification of self as male/female – arises around $2\frac{1}{2}$ yrs
- **gender role** = set of behaviours expected (by society) for a specific sex to exhibit.

Biological approach
- **physical differences** of male and female brains and hormones cause different behaviours
- hormonal effect may be while a foetus.

Suggests gender
differences in
behaviour are
INNATE.

For	Against
• There are differences between male and female hormones and physical features	• Tomboyish behaviour in adrenogenital syndrome could be due to expectations
• **testicular feminising syndrome** in Batista family – genetically male but developed female genitalia – male genitalia developed at puberty, accepted new gender	• **Mrs Went** – genetically male but testosterone insensitive – normal female life
• Money and Ehrhardt ('72) **adrenogenital syndrome** – genetic females received male hormones prenatally, later behaviour 'tomboyish'	• genetic sex and gender are not always the same – suggests there may be more to it

Biosocial approach
- **interaction between biological and social factors** (Money and Ehrhardt ('72))
- biological characteristics are used to identify sex of child, responded to differently
- gender identity initially flexible, becomes set at about $2\frac{1}{2}$ yrs (critical/sensitive period?)

For	Against
• **adrenogenital syndrome** girls reared as boys, no problem if surgical correction carried out before 3 yrs old (Money and Ehrhardt ('72)) learned gender causes problems, not genes	• Diamond ('68) most studies are of abnormal individuals – may be more flexible
• Money ('74) identical twins, one in circumcision accident, reared as girl – showed feminine behaviours though	

Social Learning Theory
- **reinforcement**, **observation** and **imitation** important
- child showing sex-appropriate behaviour will be rewarded and repeat that behaviour
- sex-inappropriate behaviour is punished and is less likely to be repeated.

For
- Bandura et al. ('61) boys more likely than girls to imitate male model
- Smith and Lloyd ('78) blue baby bounced and stimulated, pink baby soothed and given soft toys
- Sears et al. ('57) boys reinforced for being assertive, fighting back – girls punished
- Williams ('86) intro. of TV correlated with more stereotypical beliefs about gender role

Against
- Maccoby and Jacklin ('74) little evidence for more imitation of same sex
- Williams' study is correlational – could be another factor involved

Psychoanalytic Approach
- **Freud** – resolution of the Oedipus complex results in development of gender identity
- identification with same-sex parent – take on attitudes and values
- occurs during phallic stage (3–5/6 yrs)
- lack of same-sex parent may lead to homosexuality.

For
- Hetherington ('72) early loss (<4yrs) of father linked to gender role problems, later not so

Against
- no evidence that being raised in atypical household leads to atypical psychosexual development, e.g. Hoeffer ('81), Green ('78), Golombok et al. ('83)

Gender-schema theory
- **children develop schemas for genders based on experience**
- gender schemas used to organise information and can affect interpretation of events
- individual's behaviours are flexible, depending on schemas – allows for androgynous behaviours – androgynous have higher self-esteem and are more adaptable (Bem ('75)).

For
- Martin and Halverson ('81) 5/6 yr olds distort memories of gender-inconsistent behaviours
- explains development of gender behaviours before gender identity

Against
- no mention of biological factors

Cognitive-developmental theory (Kohlberg (1966))
- as cognition becomes more complex so does understanding of gender – 3 stages:
- **basic gender identity** – 2–3½ yrs – recognises self as boy/girl
- **gender identity** – 3½–4½ yrs – realisation that gender is fixed
- **gender constancy** – 4½–7 yrs – realisation that gender-inappropriate behaviours do not affect gender – not dependent on appearances.

For	Against
• Martin and Little ('90) stages occur in this order	• Maccoby ('80) gender role stereotypes learned before attentiveness to same sex
• Munroe et al. ('84) similar cross-cultural evidence	

3.3 Theories of the development of the self

self = self-concept = overall self-awareness
3 components to self: **self-image**; **self-esteem**; **ideal self**
self-esteem greater the smaller the difference between self-image and ideal self.

Social-interaction (Mead (1934))
• used ideas of 'I' and 'me' as distinct from one another
• 'I' = subject, self as knower; 'me' = object, self as known
• looking-glass self – self is understood through reactions of others – Cooley ('02)
• eventually, generalised other's viewpoint considered, not just specific
• self adapts and changes continuously – process rather than fixed structure.

Development of "self" and "others" is simultaneous.

Psychosocial development (Erikson (1968))
• development of self-understanding **through life**
• only part of a theory of **lifespan development**
• self defined in terms of **norms and values of society**.

Adolescence important in defining self.

Cognitive-developmental approach
• **self-recognition** – development of bodily self and recognition
  visual self-recognition using rouge dots (Lewis and Brooks-Gunn ('79))
• **categorical self** – social categories used for self and others, e.g. gender; age
• **psychological (private) self** – 3–4 yrs can distinguish between body and psychological self
• **self in middle childhood/adolescence** – understanding that self is not the same in all situations, also that inner qualities are part of self.

4 stages of self.

Social learning approach (Argyle (1983))
• biggest changes take place in childhood, but continue throughout life
  i.   **reaction of others** – looking-glass self (Cooley ('02))
       self-fulfilling prophecy – do as others expect
       self-esteem has effect on expectations – high expect to do well, and do (Coopersmith ('67))
  ii. **comparison with others** – many descriptors nonsense without comparisons, e.g. tall, thin
       Bannister and Agnew ('76) self is bipolar – self implies existence of non-self
  iii. **social roles** – roles become more important part of self with age – Kuhn ('60) 5/20 self descriptors for 7 yr olds, 10/20 for undergraduates
  iv. **identification with models** – identification with and imitation of models plays major part in construction of self-image – lower self-esteem more likely to imitate.

4 factors influencing the development of self – concept.

Section 3

1. List the theories of moral development.

2. Outline Kohlberg's theory of moral development.

3. Evaluate Freud's theory of moral development.

4. Outline the social learning theory of moral development and provide one piece of evidence for it.

5. List the theories of the development of gender.

6. Provide three pieces of evidence for and against the biological approach to gender development.

7. Outline the gender-schema theory of gender development.

8. Provide evidence for and against the social learning theory explanation of gender development.

9. List the theories of the development of the self.

10. Outline the social interaction model and social learning approach to self development.

4 Adolescence, adulthood and old age

4.1 Changes in adolescence

The transition period from child to adult is referred to as adolescence.

Biological approach
- the **body changes** dramatically during adolescence
- this requires **adjustments to the body image**, and therefore self-image
- **physical** changes are caused by hormonal changes controlled by the pituitary gland
- adolescents are **more aware** of what their bodies look like (Arnoff and Damianopoulos ('62))
- Jones and Bayley ('50) early developing boys more confident etc., also when older.

Psychodynamic approach

- sexual needs and reworking of old conflicts lead to **emotional upheaval** and mood swings
- two new ego defence mechanisms develop: **asceticism** (deprivation of pleasurable); **intellectualisation** (discussion of worrying topics)
- Blos ('67) must **disengage from the family** in order to form a strong relationship outside the family – reworking of old conflicts enables disengagement
- if disengagement does not occur **cannot form meaningful relationships** with outsiders.

Role-transition (identity crisis)
- Erikson ('68) included adolescence (12–18 yrs) as 1 stage in lifespan development theory
- psychological conflict to be resolved = **identity vs role confusion**

- **role transitions cause conflicts of identity** – must adapt to new roles but retain identity
- if overwhelmed by number of roles and demands – **identity diffusion** results
- identity diffusion has four parts: **intimacy**; **time**; **industry**; **negative identity**
- adolescence is a period of **psychosocial moratorium** – can play at various roles for a time
- Marcia ('66) also considers **identity crisis** important – four types of identity status as adolescent (not necessarily in order): **identity diffusion**; **identity foreclosure**; **identity moratorium**; **identity achievement**
- Marcia ('66) adolescents in id. diffusion had lower self-esteem than in id. achievement
- but – minority of US adolescents go through identity crisis (Offer ('69))
- Siddique and May ('84) 3/4 adolescents show fairly smooth transition.

Recapitulation theory – storm and stress

- Hall (1904) **ontogeny recapitulates phylogeny** (development of an individual follows the development of the species)
- adolescence is the equivalent of barbarism and tribal rivalry/warfare
- Masterton ('67) 65% adolescents showed anxiety
- but – adolescent stress could be caused by parental stress as child is changing
- Rutter et al. ('76) many adolescent problems were ongoing from childhood
- Mead ('28) more open cultures do not show storm and stress adolescence.

Coleman's (1974) focal theory

- adolescents may have more than one '**task**' to deal with at once, so focus on one and leave others until a later time
- focus on most important task at the moment
- 'task' could be dealing with **school demands**, **body changes**, altered family **relationships**
- order for tasks is not set, nor are ages, and will depend on individual
- Coleman and Hendry ('90) different anxieties most common at particular ages, large overlaps.

4.2 Changes in adulthood

Erikson (1968) 8 ages of man

- each stage has a psychological conflict to be resolved
- **young adulthood** (20s) – **intimacy vs isolation** – ability to develop trusting relationships or avoid them
- **mature adulthood** (30s–50s) – **generativity vs stagnation** – a productive and creative life or a lack of psychological development and boredom
- **late adulthood** (50s+) – **integrity vs despair** – satisfaction about life so far or feeling that life has been futile.

Problems

- **gender differences not accounted for** – Gilligan ('82) model focuses on male patterns, Hodgson and Fisher ('79) women may achieve intimacy (stage 6) before identity (stage 5)
- **individual differences not accounted for**.

Levinson (1978) 8 seasons of adulthood

- seasons only imply **change, not progression**
- periods of **transition** where major eras (early, middle and late adulthood) overlap
- seven seasons related to adulthood – first season is childhood and adolescence
- **early adult transition (17–22yrs)** – increasing independence, life choices explored
- **22–28yrs** = entering the adult world
- **29–33yrs** = age 30 transition
- **34–40yrs** = settling down
- **mid-life transition (41–45yrs)** – may be a period of mid-life crisis if goals not achieved
- **46–50yrs** = entering middle adulthood
- **51–55yrs** = age 50 transition
- **56–60yrs** = culmination of middle adulthood
- **late adult transition (61–65yrs)** – obvious physical decline cannot be ignored
- **65+yrs** = late adulthood – can be crisis time, acceptance of life and what it holds for future.

Problems

- **gender bias** towards men in Levinson's original research, but later research on women has resulted in similar patterns
- Roberts and Newton ('87) women may develop occupation later than early adulthood
- Levinson's research based on **clinical interviews** – difficult to analyse and interpret.

Gould (1978) Evolution of adult consciousness

- developed from questionnaire responses of white middle-class 16–50 yr olds
- each stage has **false assumptions** which must be dealt with:

late teens to early twenties	**I will always belong to my parents and believe in their world**
	more independence = disaster; only parents guarantee safety
twenties	**Doing things my parents' way with willpower and perseverance will bring results. If unable to cope they will step in.**
	1 right way to do things; if do what supposed to will be rewarded
late twenties to early thirties	**Life is simple and controllable. No significant contradictory forces within me.**
	I am not like my parents in ways I don't want to be
mid-thirties to fifties	**There is no evil in me or death in the world. The sinister has been destroyed.**
	work/relationships provide immunity from death

Problems

- **cannot generalise** from white middle-class 16–50 yr olds
- questionnaire generated using **inexperienced** students' ratings of taped therapy sessions.

4.3 Adjustment to old age

Disengagement theory (Cumming and Henry 1961)
- **social theory**
- gradual **separation/disengagement** from social roles and world affairs
- become more self-reliant, lose contact with others.

Problems
- Havinghurst et al. ('68) active individuals are often happiest
- may be **cohort effect** and later generations may not show this behaviour
- **cultural bias** – does not explain non-western societies.

Activity theory (Havinghurst et al. 1968)
- **social theory**
- individuals **remain active** in later life, new interests may be taken up
- **role-count** – individuals are aware of number of social roles they play
- some disengagement inevitable but more active **cope** better.

Problems
- ignores **individual differences**
- **oversimplified** account of successful ageing.

Social exchange theory (Dowd 1975)
- increased leisure time gained in **exchange** for reduced role in society.

Erikson (1963) eight ages of man
- late adulthood = 8th stage
- crisis to be resolved = **integrity vs despair** (see Section 4.2)
- **evaluation** of life so far results in satisfaction or regret and fear of death.

4 stages.

Bias.

Many individuals resist disengagement.

Positive view of ageing.

Old age is another developmental stage.

Changes in old age

Physical changes
- we become physically weaker with age – brittle bones, less elastic joints
- health and fitness are valued in society so many older people disregarded.

Retirement
- major life change, requires much adjustment (takes a long time)
- Atchley ('76) 7 phases of retirement: pre-retirement; work disengagement; honeymoon; disenchantment; reorientation; adjusted; final.

Ability
- decline in ability often exaggerated – fits stereotype
- cross-sectional studies show systematic decline in ability with age
- longitudinal studies show that decline in ability depends on how individuals use abilities
- IQ – cross-sectional studies show peak about 30yrs, longitudinal study of teachers showed increase with age (Burns ('66)) – practice and experience important
- STM and reaction time decline with age (Welford ('58))
- motivation may affect ability test scores – better on LTM and expert memory (Kimmel ('90)).

4.4 Life events in adulthood

Measuring the impact of life events

- the Holmes and Rahe ('67) **stressful life-events scale** used to measure the impact of life events – scores in 'life change units' (max. = death of spouse = 100, pregnancy (12th) = 40)
- total LCU for the last year compared with stress and illness measures – 300+ LCU are associated with serious health problems, 100+ with health problems – correlations found were small, but statistically significant
- Strack et al. ('90) stressful life-events may affect subjective well-being
- **ignores individual differences** in coping skills and 'mediating variables' such as health.

Mid-life crisis
- Sheehy ('76) occurs in 40s or 50s – important transition period
- anxiety as realisation that growing older, evaluate life so far
- Mann ('80) crisis = realisation that may not achieve goals set when younger
- 'crisis' aspect has been criticised, e.g. Brim ('76).

Parenthood
- pregnancy scores 40 LCU and gain of new family member scores 39 LCU
- social life alters – friends change, possible job change, contact with new agencies
- causes stress – Hultsch and Deutsch ('81) first child is judged as crisis event by 50–80%
- middle-class parents more disillusioned than working class – expectations? (Russell ('74))
- empty-nest period often associated with mid-life crisis.

Bereavement
- 100 LCU for death of spouse, 63 for close family member
- recent widows more likely to die (Hinton ('67))
- Ramsay ('77) grief has several components: shock; disorganisation; denial; depression; guilt; anxiety; aggression; resolution; re-integration
- Parkes ('72) three overlapping 'stages' of bereavement: denial; pining; depression
- Parkes ('72) abnormally long grieving associated with long periods of denial initially
- Parkes and Weiss ('83) abnormal grieving associated with suppression of feelings or lacking someone to talk to about it
- in Western cultures, death is often not talked about – does not help grieving process.

Some cultures revere old for wisdom they hold.

Decline in ability often exaggerated – fits stereotype.

A major life event can affect a number of areas, e.g. health, self-esteem, social life.

Major changes may occur – change job/friends.

Self-image alters as new social role.

Self-image alters as social role changes.

similar effects to death in some ways — grief, anger

47 LCU if fired, 38 if change in financial status

Questions

Test yourself — then check your answers.

Divorce

- 73 LCU for divorce, 65 for marital separation, 45 for reconciliation
- self image alters as social roles change
- division of possessions (and children!) is stressful and painful
- increased levels of illness in divorced (Carter and Glick ('70)).

Unemployment

- self image affected by major social role changes, totally different daily routine
- increased illness and psychological problems (Warr ('78))
- Argyle ('89) phases of response: shock and anger; optimistic job-seeking; pessimism; fatalism.

Section 4

1. List the explanations for the changes in adolescence.

2. Outline the role-transition explanation for changes in adolescence.

3. Assess the recapitulation theory as an explanation of changes in adolescence.

4. List the main features of the focal theory of change in adolescence.

5. List the theories of changes in adulthood.

6. What are the features of the major eras of adulthood (Levinson's model)?

7. What are the problems with Erikson's eight ages of man theory?

8. Outline the evolution of the adult consciousness model.

9. List the theories of adjustment to old age.

10. Outline the activity theory of adjustment to old age.

11. State the problems with the disengagement theory of adjustment to old age.

12. List the changes that occur with old age.

13. List some of the important life events that may occur during adulthood.

14. How can the impact of life events be measured?

15. Assess the effect of bereavement.

Chapter seven

Perspectives

1 | Approaches to psychology

1.1 Major theoretical orientations

There are a number of different approaches used in psychology, each has a different way of explaining human behaviour and makes different assumptions.

In addition to the three approaches below, others include the **information processing approach**, **ethological approach** and **developmental approach**.

Behaviourist approach

Key points
- **observable behaviours** recorded and analysed
- behaviour explained in terms of **stimulus-response** (S-R) links via learning theory
- **S-R reflexes are automatic** and unconscious
- importance of **association, reinforcement, punishment, shaping, contiguity** and **frequency**
- Watson ('13) - first used 'behaviourist', Pavlov – classical conditioning, Watson and Raynor – Little Albert, Thorndike – instrumental learning, Skinner – operant conditioning.

Practical applications
- **classroom management** – reward desirable behaviour only (Wheldall and Merrett ('83))
- **programmed learning** – step-by-step learning, reward as each correct response noted
- **token economy** – for behaviour modification, tokens = secondary reinforcers (reward)
- **biofeedback** – control of heart rate, blood pressure etc.
- **clinical applications** – systematic desensitisation, implosion therapy, aversion therapy.

For	Against
• uses scientific methodology – testable	• deterministic – human behaviour is caused by environment
• learning theory is wide-reaching – has been used to explain many aspects of psychology	• reductionist – all behaviours reduced to S-R links
• in humans, rewards may be intrinsic rather than extrinsic	• most research on animals
	• based on observable events only

Humanistic approach

Key points
- directly **opposed** to deterministic behaviourist and psychodynamic approaches
- each individual has **innate potential** and aims to fulfil potential (intuition of what is best)
- **positive view** of human beings
- importance of **self-esteem, subjective experience, self-control** (*free will*), **need fulfilment** and **awareness of own needs**
- Maslow – hierarchy of needs, Rogers – personality development.

Classical and operant conditioning = learning theory (Chapter 2, Section 4.1).

Individual-based approach.

Practical applications
- **humanistic psychotherapy** – external pressures may prevent individual need fulfilment – unhealthy and unproductive – help individuals to resist pressures
- **development of qualitative research methods**.

For	Against
• highlights limitations of traditional explanations of human behaviour	• need fulfilment advocates selfishness – not always observed
	• no universal right – since only an individual knows what is best for them

Psychodynamic approach

Key points
- **conscious** and **unconscious** aspects of mind
- three parts to personality, develop in sequence:
  id = self-gratification, in unconscious mind
  ego = considers consequences of actions, mainly conscious mind
  superego = conscience, results in socially acceptable behaviour, mainly conscious mind
- **five psychosexual stages** of development: **oral** (<15mth); **anal** (15mth–3yr); **phallic** (3–5yr); **latency** (5yr–puberty); **genital** (puberty onwards)
- importance of repression, denial, displacement, projection (ego defence mechanisms)
- used to explain moral and gender development, aggression, prejudice, forgetting.

> Resolution of conflicts for progression.

Practical applications
- **psychotherapy** – adult neuroses due to unresolved conflicts in childhood
- **play therapy** in children, e.g. Dibs.

For	Against
• stresses importance of childhood for later life	• mind-body causal link is disputed
• identifies unconscious influences	• untestable – no predictive hypotheses, merely descriptive
• extremely influential theory	

1.2 Debates concerning the nature of the person

Free will vs determinism

- **free will** – an individual is able to choose own behaviour regardless of past experience
- **determinism** – an individual's behaviour is determined by internal or external events
- Heather ('76) free to choose from limited range of behaviours
- **humanist approach** – individuals free to choose actions, plan destiny – have ultimate responsibility for own actions.

> Absolute free will is unlikely – experience affects us.

Types of determinism
- **causal determinism** – behaviour determined by goal to be achieved (not past events) so individual is free to choose, since chooses goal – compatible with free will
- **environmental determinism** – behaviourist approach – conditioning determines our behaviours, environment causes behaviours to occur (Skinner ('71))
- **biological determinism** – internal factors (e.g. hormones) determine behaviour
- **genetic determinism** – innate factors determine behaviour
- **psychic determinism** – psychodynamic approach – behaviour controlled by unconscious forces.

> Causal determinism is compatible with free will.

Science and determinism

- science aims to identify cause and effect, i.e. determinants of behaviours
- can use determinants to predict behaviours – emphasis on past events affecting future
- maybe more emphasis needed on causal determinism.

Moral issues

- **free will** – individual holds ultimate responsibility for antisocial actions – assumed by law
- **determinism** – situation (or genes, hormones, unconscious etc.) caused behaviour – individual cannot be held responsible since not in control of own actions.

b. Reductionism

- complex event can be reduced to simpler component processes
- simplest level of explanation is the best.

Types of reductionism

- **physiological reductionism** – behaviour explained by physiology, e.g. hormones
- **evolutionary reductionism** – behaviours have evolved because they have 'survival value' – useful to study simpler animals since common ancestor and share behaviour patterns
- **environmental reductionism** – behaviourist approach – behaviour explained by S-R links
- **machine reductionism** – information processing approach – behaviour explained by input-throughput-output – similarity with computers.

For	Against
• easy to test hypotheses and theories using scientific method	• does not consider whole behaviour
• may be essential to understand behaviour in simplest terms before explaining whole	• studying one aspect at a time gives biased view
	• whole greater than sum of its parts

- Rose ('76) may be several levels of explanation of behaviour – sociological, social, psychological, physiological, anatomical-biochemical, chemical, physical – any behaviour can be explained in variety of ways depending on level of explanation used.

Questions

Test yourself – then check your answers.

Section 1

1. What are the major theoretical orientations in psychology?

2. Give the main features of the behaviourist approach to psychology.

3. State 2 advantages and disadvantages of the behaviourist approach.

4. Decribe the practical applications of the humanistic approach.

5. Outline the main points of the psychodynamic approach to psychology.

6. State the limitations and advantages of the psychodynamic approach.

7. What is free will?

8. What is determinism?

9. Name five types of determinism.

10. What is the humanist stance on the free will vs determinism debate?

11. What is the behaviourist stance on the free will vs determinism debate?

12. What is the psychodynamic stance on the free will vs determinism debate?

13. How does science fit into the free will vs determinism debate?

14. Explain how free will vs determinism has moral implications.

15. What are the assumptions of reductionism?

16. Name 4 types of reductionism.

17. What are the advantages and limitations of reductionism?

2 Controversies in psychology

2.1 'Controversial' applications of psychological research

Advertising

There are several areas where psychology can be applied to advertising.

- psychological research has been used to make advertisements as persuasive as possible
- psychologists should be aware that their research can have practical applications
- adverts often portray potentially harmful situations positively – ethical implications.

Need – Persuading people they have a need for a particular product.
- **familiarity** – more likely to buy familiar brand, adverts make brands familiar
- **association** – adverts are happy, funny etc. (US), produce positive feelings (UCR) associated with the product (CS), repeated presentation leads to **classical conditioning** – product becomes associated with positive feelings
- **confirmatory bias** – stereotypical images used to indicate situations when product would be used – happy housewife, people with jobs etc.

Attracting attention

Bypass analytical left hemisphere.

- many adverts designed to appeal to emotions – right hemisphere of brain
- linked with association and classical conditioning (see above).

Remembering product
- repetition does not always improve memory for product, imagery and information used too
- jingles can increase cued recall – useful when cues present, e.g. on supermarket shelf
- adverts in 'happy' programmes are better remembered.

Purchase
- fast-marketing (issuing free samples) – more likely to change attitude about product.

Post-purchase
- inaction by consumer means most likely to repeat purchase
- **post-decisional dissonance** – seek out adverts for product bought to reinforce decision.

Propaganda and warfare

Psychological techniques have been applied to propaganda, persuasion and interrogation.

- **propaganda** – disguised, selected (one-sided) information is used to induce certain attitudes
- **persuasion** – Petty and Cacioppo ('81) **elaboration likelihood model** – 2 routes:
  central route – 'solid' argument, motivated to think about issue, become persuaded
  peripheral route – use peripheral features – like advertising – less stable, attitude change

- **coercive persuasion** ('brainwashing') – individual's ability to reason is suppressed Schein ('56) **Korean POWs** – i. unfreeze existing attitudes via deprivation; ii. replace attitudes via persuasion; iii. refreeze new attitudes via reward system
- **warfare** – psychological techniques used to undermine morale of enemy – often leaflets, e.g. American propaganda in Vietnam, Nazi propaganda in Holland
- **psychological warfare** – dehumanisation via desensitisation to violence, **psychological brutality** (less visible damage), targeting values of enemy
- **interrogation** techniques – sensory deprivation; ask impossible questions then a real one; silence implies compliance; vague threats.

Psychometric testing

Used to **measure ability/personality trait**, compare to other scores.
Good tests must be *valid*, *reliable* (see Chapter 8, Section 2.8) and **standardised** (norm and criterion referencing).

Personality testing
- to measure attitudes, emotions, motivation etc. often for career or personnel selection
- e.g. 16PF test (Cattell et al. ('70)), EPQ (Eysenck personality questionnaire)
- often yes/no answers to questions so easy to collect and score, quantities of data.

Problems
- can give **fake answers** to enhance scores (increased *social desirability*) or answer yes to everything (**acquiescence**)
- tests often **biased by personality theory** used to generate them
- **forced-choice** questions give limited information
- used to make **important decisions**, e.g. career choice, job suitability.

Intelligence testing
- used to measure **intellectual capacity**
- IQ (intelligence quotient) test – written test adjusted for age
- **Watson-Glaser critical thinking appraisal** – graduate recruitment
- **Weschler intelligence scale for children (WISC)** – oral test
- some non-verbal tests, e.g. part of WISC.

Problems
- **test bias** (see Chapter 6, Section 2.3) – test may be biased towards specific culture or theory, e.g. Black children score lower on IQ test, but white children score lower on BITCH test
- **individual differences** may be due to anxiety in test conditions rather than different abilities
- used to make **important decisions**, e.g. suitability for job/school.

Generally, psychometric tests are cost-effective and easy to administer with some predictive validity – but over-reliance on test scores is not productive – they do not guarantee success and are not always an accurate measure of ability/attitude.

2.2 Psychology as a science

What is a science?
- use of **empirical observation** to produce **testable theories** – cyclic model (see figure 7.1)
- Slife and Williams ('95) observations are objective and under controlled conditions, predictions can be made and tested, methods and results can be replicated
- Kuhn ('70) single paradigm encompassing all research (science evolves through pre-science (no paradigm), science (paradigm), revolution (paradigm rejected)).

Many personality tests have predictive validity.

Imply fixed personality.

Narrow definition of intelligence.

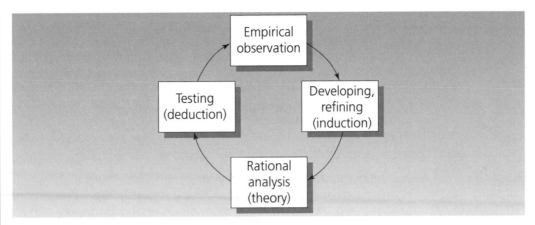

Figure 7.1 Cyclic model

Is psychology a science?

For

- *cyclic model* used – theories generated from objective observations, tested and adjusted
- much methodology is *objective and under controlled* conditions to establish cause and effect

Against

- *no single paradigm* universally accepted by psychologists
- methods and results often *not repeatable* – demand characteristics, sample bias etc.
- may not be entirely objective – *experimenter bias*
- correlational studies cannot determine cause and effect

Should human behaviour be studied scientifically?

- depends on aspect of human behaviour – seems appropriate for cognitive psychology, also bio-psychology – but social and abnormal psychology much less suited to scientific method
- human behaviour is complex but scientific method is reductionist and determinist
- human behaviour occurs in the real world, scientific method lacks ecological validity
- restricted samples produce culturally and socially biased results
- but – scientific method is required if theories are to be tested
- **methodological pluralism** required for study of human behaviour.

Scientific methods more suitable for some areas of psychology than others.

2.3 Biases in theory and research

Cultural diversity

Hofstede ('80) culture = 'pre-programming of the mind which distinguishes members of one group from another'.

NB – if 2 cultures differ, 2 individuals from cultures not necessarily show biases.

Imposed etic affects all research, and most research is by western researchers on western participants.

Emic–etic distinction

- **emic = culturally specific** human behaviour
- **etic = universal** (e.g. has been suggested for moral and cognitive development)
- **imposed etic** – explanations for behaviours observed in one culture used for all cultures
- e.g. IQ testing, moral development theories, prejudice testing – F scale Adorno et al. ('50)
- Berry ('69) **derived etic** – series of culture specific (emic) studies.

Cross-cultural research
- often used to identify innate, universal behaviours (e.g. perceptual development)
- but – mis-interpretation possible – particularly of language, but also actions
- imposed etic possible – particularly as cultural biases affect interpretation of observations
- often small sample – not representative of whole culture, may be sub-culture.

Ethnocentrism
- most psychological research carried out on white, male, middle-class, European undergraduates – provides a very restricted sample
- also, most research carried out by a similar group – Western views are predominant
- e.g. self – Western research emphasis on independence and individuality, Africans (over-generalisation, again) value co-operation much more
- e.g. IQ test – Blacks seen as inferior (Jensen ('69)) due to lower scores, but test bias.

Gender

Differences
- Maccoby ('80) differences within sexes as great as differences between
- differences may be due to biological differences or socialisation
- **nb** – research that does not find differences is less likely to be published.

Bias in theories
- **alpha-biased** emphasise gender differences, e.g. Freud and moral development
- **beta-biased** ignore gender differences – based on research with one gender, assumed to be true for both – e.g. males – Asch (conformity), females – Hofling et al. (obedience).

Bias in research
- **androcentric** – male behaviour studied, assumed to be normal human behaviour – female behaviour may be classified as abnormal, e.g. Kohlberg and moral development
- Nicholson ('95) experimental method disadvantages women by placing in unnatural situation, responding to male researcher (usually)
- variables may be defined in male-biased ways, e.g. leader = aggressive, dominant.

Feminist psychology
- much psychological research has **imposed etic**
- Bem ('93) **enculturated lens theory** – male interpretations of female behaviours – seen as abnormal, e.g. pre-menstrual syndrome.

Non-westerners are "invisible" to research and theory.

Research has often ignored women – they are "invisible".

Adult behaviours usually = male behaviours.

Questions

Test yourself – then check your answers.

Section 2

1. List the five main areas of application of psychology to advertising.

2. Explain how conditioning techniques can be used in advertising.

3. What is propaganda?

4. What are the three stages in coercive persuasion?

5. How can psychological techniques be used in warfare?

6. What is a psychometric test?

7. State the three main advantages of psychometric testing.

8. Give four problems associated with the use of personality tests and intelligence tests.

9. What is meant by 'science'?

10. Describe Kuhn's definition of science in terms of paradigm.

11. What are the main arguments for and against psychology being a science?

12. How appropriate is the scientific method in psychology?

13. What is an imposed etic?

14. Give examples, in psychology, where an imposed etic is a concern.

15. What problems may arise with cross-cultural research?

16. Why might ethnocentrism be a problem in psychology?

17. In what ways can research and theories be gender biased?

18. How are differences between the sexes overemphasised?

3 | Ethical issues in psychology

Originally, individual psychologists were expected to consider ethical issues. Later, guidelines were drawn up for use by all, e.g. British Psychological Society (BPS) guidelines ('90), American Psychological Association (APA) guidelines.

3.1 Use of human participants in psychological investigations

BPS ethical principles for research with human participants:
- **general – mutual respect and confidence** required between researcher and participant – and must eliminate threats to psychological well-being, health, values and dignity
- **consent – full disclosure** of objectives of investigation required for participant to give informed consent
  cannot be obtained with some observational studies, field experiments and with children
- **deception** – informed consent cannot be gained, but behaviour may be affected if deception not used due to participant expectations
  deception not acceptable for trivial investigations (ends justify means)
  prior general consent – participants consent to deception, e.g. Gamson et al. ('82)
- **debriefing** – vital, particularly if deception involved – inform of true nature of investigation, participants should leave study in same psychological state as when arrived
- **withdrawal** – make clear that participants can withdraw at any stage
- **confidentiality** – names not used, data not identifiable as belonging to individual
- **protection** – from mental and physical harm, protect from stress
- **observational research** – if consent not obtained then only behaviour observed in public places allowed, where expect to be in view of strangers
- **giving advice** – if investigator obtains evidence of physical/psychological problem (possible danger) should inform participant and recommend appropriate advisor.

Researchers should consider ethical guidelines when designing research and not carry out studies where they expect stress to occur. During or after research, it may become evident that undue stress has occurred, e.g. Zimbardo's prison role-play was stopped prematurely, Milgram did not expect to gain the results he did. Criticism is easier with hindsight.

Research should conform to these guidelines.

You should be able to evaluate the ethics of studies.

3.2 Use of non-human animals in psychological investigations

Non-human animals are used in lab. studies and naturalistic observations.

Relevance to human behaviour

<table>
<tr><th>For</th><th>Against</th></tr>
<tr><td>

- some behaviours are the same, e.g. neurological behaviour
- evolution suggests common ancestors so common behavioural building blocks
- useful comparisons can be made – behaviourist approach
- behaviour less complex so simpler to study
- instinctive behaviours easier to study – learned behaviours less important
- greater experimental control and objectivity possible and fewer biases, expectations etc.
- animals have been used when human investigation would be impossible, e.g. Harlow's ('62) deprivation studies with rhesus monkeys – ethical problems

</td><td>

- humans are qualitatively different from animals – humanist argument
- human behaviour more reliant on cultural transmission
- anthropomorphism – may transfer human thoughts/feelings to animals
- ethical arguments – Regan and Singer ('76) no pain or distress is justifiable
- cannot determine any thought processes

</td></tr>
</table>

Shorter generation time – can study successive generations.

Similar structures do not necessarily perform same functions.

Carrying out research with animals

Laboratory research

- Animals (Scientific Procedures) Act 1986 covers use of animals in research in UK considers **ethics** (do ends justify means?)
  species used and number of animals – smallest possible number should be used
  caging and crowding – living conditions should vary depending on species
  pain or stress disallowed if alternatives possible, if used must be kept to minimum and must be fully justified – individual assessment by Home Office required
- **Bateson's ('86) decision cube** – three criteria used to assess animal research: **animal suffering**; **quality of research**; **certainty of benefit**
  only carry out research if suffering low, quality of research and certainty of benefit high.

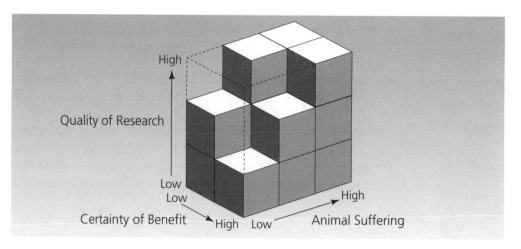

Figure 7.2 Bateson's decision cube

Field experiments

Manipulating natural environment of animals.

- manipulating natural environment of animals
- provides valid information on how animals respond to stimuli
- generally little direct benefit to humans – low justification using Bateson cube
- great responsibility not to disrupt natural habitat irreversibly
- pilot studies should be used to assess possible disturbance levels
- effects on species not in study should be assessed.

3.3. Ethical responsibilities of psychologists

Ethics of socially sensitive research

- socially sensitive research has **consequences** for groups of people represented by the participants in the research – e.g. research into 'alternative' sexuality or race
- some research may be used for **social manipulation** and therefore creates an ethical dilemma for the researcher, e.g. Hamer ('95) describes a 'gay gene', others suggested the possibility of a test for the gene so abortions could be performed on foetuses with the gene
- **race-related** research is affected by an imposed etic (Section 2.3)

Results of research may be used by other agencies – psychologists must be aware of this.

- Sieber and Stanley ('88) 4 aspects of research require consideration:
  i. **formulation of research question** – may add 'scientific dignity' to existing prejudice
  ii. **conduct of research, treatment of participants** – confidentiality important, but criminal/dangerous behaviour may allow breach of confidentiality
  iii. **institutional context** – context affects behaviour observed
  iv. **interpretation of findings** – findings may be used for unintended purposes, e.g. social control – knowledge is not necessarily ethically neutral.

Responsibilities of researcher

Researchers should conduct honest and meaningful research.

- **ethical treatment** of all participants (human and non-human)
- responsibility of research uses
- **social manipulation** – research may be used for political purposes
- **social control** – psychologists decide who is abnormal and who needs treatment
- **monitor** other researchers and *report malpractice* (BPS guidelines)
- **publish research** and provide access to data collected.

Questions

Section 3

Test yourself – then check your answers.

1. What are the main points in the BPS guidelines?

2. What is meant by 'informed consent'?

3. What is meant by 'the ends justify the means'?

4. Comment on the use of deception in psychological enquiry.

5. What are the advantages of using non-human animals in psychological investigations?

6. What are the disadvantages of using non-human animals in psychological investigations?

7. What are the main points in the Animals (Scientific Procedures) Act 1986?

8. What considerations apply to field experiments?

9. Outline the main problems of socially sensitive research.

10. What are the responsibilities of a researcher of psychology?

Chapter eight

Research methods in psychology

1 | The nature of psychological enquiry

1.1 Experimental investigations

Laboratory experiments
- experimenter **manipulates IV** to study effect on DV (causal relationship)
- **tight control** over extraneous variables
- **random allocation** of participants to experimental and control groups
- participants should not suffer stress or harm in any form
- e.g. Milgram ('63) obedience
- e.g. Broadbent ('54) attention.

For	Against
• can be replicated	• usually lack ecological validity, so cannot generalise to other situations
• do not have to wait for events to occur	• demand characteristics
• control over variables – can determine cause and effect	• experimenter effects
• can generalise if representative sample	• sampling bias
• quantitative data – analysed statistically	• ethics – often problems with deception and informed consent

Field experiments
- experiments carried out in **natural surroundings** (in the field)
- experimenter **manipulates IV**
- e.g. Sherif et al. ('61) robber's cave
- e.g. Piliavin et al. ('69) helping behaviour.

For	Against
• greater ecological validity than lab. expt. so more able to generalise	• lack of control of extraneous variables
• if naive participants – no demand characteristics or experimenter effects	• cannot generalise to other situations
	• difficult to replicate
	• ethics – informed consent not given

1.2 Quasi- and non-experimental investigations

Natural experiments
- effects of **naturally occurring IV** studied
- **quasi-experimental** (similar to experimental, but researcher does not control IV)
- can compare 'experimental' and control groups
- e.g. Williams ('86) TV, gender stereotypes and aggression
- e.g. Shields ('62) twin studies.

For	Against
• no demand characteristics or experimenter bias • can study cause and effect where ethically unsound to manipulate IV	• lack of control of variables by researcher • have to wait for situations to naturally arise • participants may realise being studied and alter behaviour accordingly

Investigations using correlational analysis

- **relationship** between two covariables calculated (e.g. height and weight) – **inferential statistic**
- if both increase together = positive correlation etc. (see Section 3.6)
- e.g. Murstein ('72) attractiveness in partners
- e.g. Williams ('86) TV and gender stereotypes and aggression.

For	Against
• strength of relationships can be calculated • can be used to study areas ethically unsound to engineer • useful preliminary study	• cannot assume cause and effect • both covariables can be affected by another, extraneous variable • non-linear relationships can be missed

Naturalistic observation

- observation of behaviour in **natural environment**
- observer remains **inconspicuous**, does not interfere with behaviour
- can be used for investigation **prior to main study**
- e.g. Lorenz ('37) imprinting in precocial animals
- e.g. Kawamura ('63) spread of learning in Japanese macaques.

Studying the effects of a natural event.

For	Against
• can study behaviours ethically unsound to engineer • high ecological validity • no demand characteristics or experimenter effects (if undetected) • useful for animals which cannot be studied in laboratory	• cannot control extraneous variables • cannot assume cause and effect • observer bias • observer may affect behaviour • inter- and intra-rater reliability • ethical issues – no informed consent • cannot replicate and cannot generalise

Case studies

- **detailed investigation** of a single individual or small group of people
- **confidentiality** of participants must be ensured
- often used in order to **plan therapy** or treatment
- e.g. amnesics – KF (Shallice and Warrington ('70))
- e.g. isolated children – Genie (Curtiss ('77)), Isabelle (Davis ('47)).

For

- can study areas unethical to artificially engineer (e.g. abuse)
- in-depth information
- high ecological validity

Against

- cannot generalise
- retrospective – memory unreliable
- bias in interpretation
- unstructured method, cannot replicate
- time-consuming

Several types of interview.

Interviews

- wide range of styles from **informal 'chat' to clinical interview** (pre-determined questions, depend on answers to previous questions)
- **confidentiality** must be ensured
- e.g. Piaget ('54) child development
- e.g. Levinson ('78) seasons of life.

For

- casual, unstructured interview can reveal realistic information not otherwise accessible
- flexibility of questioning
- clinical interviews can give an insight into the thoughts of others
- high ecological validity

Against

- difficult to generalise from unstructured
- more formal styles may intimidate participants so may not talk as freely
- bias in interpretation possible
- difficult to analyse, particularly informal
- interviewer effects
- demand characteristics

Relatively recent development.

Discourse analysis

- study of **discourse**, e.g. conversations in natural situations
- analysis of **underlying themes** and meaning – same sentence can have many meanings
- depending on who says it, to whom, and in what context – different interpretations are possible
- no one interpretation is correct
- e.g. Gavey ('92) power and coercion in heterosexual relationships.

For

- rich, qualitative data generated
- very high ecological validity

Against

- cannot generalise from specific situations
- subjective interpretation

Section 1

1. What are the characteristics of laboratory and field experiments?
2. What are the advantages and disadvantages of laboratory experiments?
3. List the quasi- and non-experimental investigation techniques.
4. What is a natural experiment? Give an example.
5. What are the advantages and disadvantages of correlational analysis?
6. What are the advantages and disadvantages of naturalistic observation?
7. What is discourse analysis?
8. What is a case study?
9. What are the advantages and disadvantages of interviews?

2 | The design and implementation of experimental and non-experimental investigations

2.1 Aims and hypotheses

- an aim states the **broad question(s)** which it is hoped will be answered by a study
- **a hypothesis is a precise, unambiguous prediction** of the findings of a study
- **null hypothesis** (H_0) = states no significant difference between control and experimental group (or no correlation) – any differences are due to chance
- **alternative/experimental hypothesis** (H_1) = states effect of IV on DV
- **one-tailed H_1** – specifies direction of effect of IV on DV (e.g. IV will cause DV to increase)
- **two-tailed H_1** – no direction specified, only that a difference will occur.

2.2 Sampling

Random
- **every individual** in target population has an **equal chance** of being selected for sample
- a random sample is not necessarily a representative sample of a population
- e.g. draw names from a hat.

Opportunity
- sample consists of those individuals **available** from target population
- **not random, probably biased** – often used because simple
- e.g. all participants are students at university or college.

Systematic
- take e.g. every 10th individual from a list of the target population
- **unbiased sample** of target population
- **not random** – not an equal chance of selecting every individual, = *quasi-random.*

Stratified
- target population is divided into **relevant groups/strata**
- **proportions** of relevant groups in sample should be the same as in target population
- e.g. target population is 80% male, 60% working class – so is sample

- selection of individuals from relevant groups in target population is **random**
- sample is **representative** of target population – **can generalise**.

Quota
- similar to **stratified** but selection of individuals is **not random**
- can be used if cannot access entire target population for sampling.

Self-selected (volunteer)
- participants **select themselves**
- e.g. reply to newspaper advertisement, fill in and return questionnaire
- **volunteer bias** – not representative of population as a whole – **cannot generalise**.

2.3 Categorising behaviour

Recording
video and audiotape often used – help reduce bias
intra- and inter-rater reliability may be a problem – checks should be made.

Structured method
- predetermined categories of behaviour often used, coding system
- some behaviours may not fit neatly into predetermined categories.

Unstructured method
- write down what happens, diary method
- more open to biased interpretation.

Sampling
- **time interval sampling** – record behaviour at fixed time intervals, e.g. every 2 mins
- **event sampling** – tally kept of every behavioural event occurring (frequency count)
- **point sampling** – record behaviour of one individual, then another.

2.4 Variables

Operational definitions of variables are very precise definitions, general terms are not used, e.g. DV should be 'number of words recalled' rather than 'memory'.

Experimental variables
Independent variable (IV) = variable manipulated by experimenter to study effect on DV, e.g. time elapsed since learned a list of words.

Dependent variable (DV) = variable being measured to see if it varies when IV is manipulated, e.g. number of words recalled.

Extraneous variables
- may obscure or artificially enhance effect of IV – **confounds results**
- **random error** – cannot be predicted, e.g. noise levels, temperature, motivation of participant
- **constant error** – has consistent effect on DV, e.g. participant differences between groups, order effects (lack of counter-balancing).

Variables other than IV, which may affect DV.

2.5 Experimental design

a. Independent groups
- separate, independent groups of participants
- one (or more) groups receive the experimental treatment = **experimental group**
- other group does not = **control group**
- 2 groups are compared for DV scores.

2 groups.

For	Against
• no order effects	• differences between groups may be due to participant variables
• participants less likely to determine purpose of experiment than with repeated measures – fewer demand characteristics	• more participants needed
	• unrelated statistical tests less powerful

b. Repeated measures
• same participants undergo experimental and control conditions – DV tested twice for each participant.

For	Against
• participant variables cannot affect results	• order effects if not counter-balanced
• fewer participants needed	• demand characteristics – participants may determine purpose of experiment
• related statistical tests more sensitive	

c. Matched participants
• separate groups of participants in experimental and control groups
• pairs of participants are matched closely for factors which may affect DV – one of pair is allocated to experimental, other to control group.

For	Against
• partial control of participant variables	• time-consuming and difficult, not all initial participants will be used
• no order effects	• participants cannot be matched exactly
• fewer demand characteristics	

2.6 Minimising situational variables

Standardisation
• standardised procedures ensure procedure cannot affect DV
• e.g. standardised instructions, equipment, observations, scoring.

Counterbalancing
• takes account of order effects in repeated measures designs (practice and fatigue effect)
• two groups: one undergoes experimental then control conditions, other vice versa
• not always possible to undergo control after experimental – use independent groups design.

Randomisation
• if several tests/items then counterbalancing is complicated
• randomised order of presentation should prevent order effects, if large enough sample.

2.7 Relationships between researchers and participants

Experimenter effect (bias)
• **expectations** of experimenter may be (unconsciously) **communicated** *to participants*
• experimental and control groups are treated slightly differently
• affects participants' behaviour, affects results

- Rosenthal ('66) students found rats learned maze quicker if expected them to
- male researchers more likely to smile at female participants – may bias results.

Hawthorne effect
- Mayo ('33) performance can improve due to increased attention participant receives.

Greenspoon effect
- Greenspoon ('55) comments by experimenter affected responses given by participants.

Demand characteristics
- the aspects of an investigation that participants use as cues to affect their behaviour
- they may use these cues to guess what the investigation is about and **behave in the appropriate manner** – Orne ('62) found this with 'sensory deprivation'
- they may deliberately **behave in an inappropriate manner**
- participants are not passive – they actively seek out information.

Reduction of bias

Single-blind condition
- **participants do not know** if they are in the experimental or control group
- **placebo** (= 'treatment' that has no effect) may be given.

Double-blind condition
- **participants and experimenter are unaware** which group the participant is in
- **experimenter bias** is not always eliminated as the experimenter is active also.

Disguising purpose
- asking a **range of questions** rather than only one being investigated in attempt to reduce participant bias – less likely to guess purpose.

2.8 Reliability and validity

Generalisability
- depends on a number of factors including: **sample size**; **sampling method**; **reliability**; **validity**; possible **biases** – demand characteristics, experimenter bias; **situational variables**; **participant variables**; **design of investigation**.

Reliability
- reliable measuring systems always give same values if measuring same item/individual.

test reliability refers to consistency of test scoring system
i. **test-retest reliability** = participant takes test twice, correlation between scores
ii. **equivalent forms** = correlation between 2 equivalent tests for same participant
iii. **split-half** = correlation between 2 halves of same test for same participant.

scorer reliability – inter-rater and intra-rater reliability
i. **inter-rater** = correlation between marks awarded by 2 different scorers marking same test.
ii. **intra-rater** = correlation between marks awarded by 1 scorer on 1 test on 2 occasions.

Validity
- **face validity** – does the test appear to be valid when judged by experts – crude and subjective
- **content validity** – experts examine all aspects of test to judge validity – still crude
- **predictive validity** – test participants' performance at a later date to check if test predicted
- **concurrent validity** – correlate participants' test scores with those on another, independent, valid test – high correlation indicates validity
- **construct validity** – test participants expected to score differently, check that they do

Reliable results can be replicated.

High correlation = high similarity = high reliability.

Valid tests measure what they are supposed to measure.

Section 2

1. What is a null hypothesis?

2. List the methods of sampling a population.

3. List methods of categorising behaviour.

4. List the different types of variables.

5. Name the different types of experimental design.

6. What are the advantages and disadvantages of a repeated measures design?

7. What are the advantages and disadvantages of a matched pairs design?

8. What methods can be used to minimise situational variables?

9. List the biases that may arise due to the researcher–participant relationship.

10. How may researcher–participant biases be reduced?

11. What are the different types of reliability?

12. How can reliability be tested?

13. Outline the different types of validity and how they are measured.

Test yourself –
then check
your answers.

3 | Data analysis

3.1 Content analysis

High ecological
validity.

- **indirect, observational technique** – analysis of forms, books, magazines, TV, video etc.
- often count frequency of use of words/behaviours of interest
- **quantitative data** can be produced
- but – **subjectivity** of scoring can be a problem
- may result in **incomplete analysis** since interrelationships of events can be ignored.

3.2 Interpretation of interviews, case studies and observation

Analysis of this type of research is usually qualitative.

Analysis of interviews
- **quantitative data** is only likely from structured interviews – analysed using statistics
- **qualitative data** can be analysed and presented in various ways
- organisation of interview responses by themes or questions asked
- present quotations to illustrate key points
- **high ecological validity** if unstructured, but **low reliability**
- analysis is *difficult* and can be subjective.

Analysis of case studies
- description of events occurring is needed
- descriptions of events/feelings recalled by participant are *affected by interpretation*
- interpretation of events by researcher should be made explicit where it occurs
- **potential for biased reporting** – only report items that fit with theory
- **cannot be replicated so low reliability**.

Analysis of observations
- **quantitative data** (from event sampling etc.) can be analysed using statistical techniques

High ecological
validity.

- careful **categorisation** of behaviours required for quantitative analysis
- **qualitative data** can be presented in various ways
- descriptions of actual behaviours (care needed not to interpret)
- must be clear when interpretations of researcher are being presented
- usually **high ecological validity** – inappropriate categories cause problems.

3.3 Measures of central tendency

Descriptive
statistics.

- show the middle of the data in various ways
- **mode** – most frequently occurring value, the highest point on a frequency distribution graph. Use with bimodal distributions, nominal data. Simple, gives no info. about other values
- **median** – middle value when all values arranged in ascending/descending order. Use with non-normal distributions of interval data, or ordinal data. Little affected by extreme values
- **mean** – arithmetic mean – add up all values and divide by number of values (N). Only use with normal distributions of interval data. Highly affected by extreme value.

3.4 Measures of dispersion

Descriptive
statistics.

- the bigger the values calculated, the more spread out (dispersed) the data
- **variation ratio** – percentage of non-modal scores. Use with mode, also simple
- **range** – difference between lowest and highest value. Affected by extreme values. Minimal information about data set as a whole
- **standard deviation (s)** – Use only with normal distributions of interval data. Highly affected by skewed data. Most accurate measure since all values are taken into account
- *variance (s^2)* – standard deviation squared.

3.5 Graphical representations

bar charts – suitable for nominal data, bars have gaps between them (Fig. 8.1)

histograms – use with interval/ordinal data, no gaps between bars (Fig. 8.2)

frequency polygons – as for histograms but join up mid-point of each bar (Fig. 8.3).

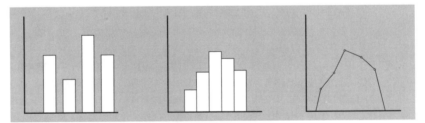

Fig 8.1 Bar chart   *Fig 8.2 Histogram*   *Fig 8.3 Frequency polygon*

scattergraphs – used for correlational data, if both variables increase together = positive correlation, if 1 increases as other decreases = negative, no line of best fit = no correlation.

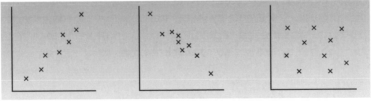

Fig 8.4 positive correlation   *Fig 8.5 negative correlation*   *Fig 8.6 no correlation*

3.6 Two sample statistical tests of difference, association and correlation

These are inferential statistical tests.

Tests of difference

(Mann-Whitney U, Wilcoxon, Sign, Chi-squared)
Compare the 2 data sets and calculate the probability that they both come from the same population.

Unrelated data

Mann-Whitney U test
- comparing two unrelated (independent) sets of data
- used with ordinal, interval or ratio data
- powerful test, can be used with small sample sizes
- correction needed if either sample is >20.

Chi-squared test
- compares observed frequencies with expected frequencies for independent data
- Chi-squared should only be used for nominal data, if frequencies have been recorded.
- if the expected values in any cell is <5 the test becomes less reliable.

Related data

Wilcoxon matched pairs signed ranks test
- comparing two related sets of data (from repeated/related measures design)
- used with ordinal, interval or ratio data
- powerful test, can be used with small sample sizes – correction needed if sample >25 pairs.

Sign test
- tests direction of a difference between pairs of values (e.g. larger/smaller after treatment?)
- limited information given, size of difference not indicated
- used with nominal data.

Tests of association or correlation

(Spearman's rho, Chi-squared)
they calculate a measure of how the two variables covary.

Spearman's rho
- used with ordinal, interval or ratio data – used with pairs of scores
- data can be visualised using a scattergraph
- **+1 = perfect positive** correlation, all points on straight line, as A increases so does B
- **–1 = perfect negative** correlation, all points on straight line, as A increases B decreases
- **0 = no correlation**
- values in between 0 and +/–1 show varying degrees of correlation between variables
- also, a probability level (p) may be calculated, if $p \leq 0.05$ we can reject the null hypothesis.

Chi-squared test (see above)
- simply tests if two variables associated, e.g. is gender associated with aggression?
- If $p \leq 0.05$, we reject the null hypothesis and accept the alternative – there is an association.

When to use each test

	scale of measurement	
	ratio/interval/ ordinal data	nominal data
independent measures	Mann-Whitney U test	Chi-squared test
repeated measures	Wilcoxon	Sign test
correlation	Spearman's rho	Chi-squared test

3.7 Statistical significance

Inferential statistical tests (of difference or association/correlation) result in a **probability level (p)** being calculated. The value of p indicates the probability that the data were generated by chance. The lower the value of p, the less likely it is that the results were due to chance, and the more certain we can be about rejecting the null hypothesis.

- if $p \leq 0.01$, there is less than (or equal to) a 1 in 100 likelihood (1%) that the results were generated by chance (i.e. not very likely) – reject the null, highly significant

- if $p \leq 0.05$, there is less than (or equal to) a 1 in 20 likelihood (5%) that the results were generated by chance – reject the null, significant

- if $p \leq 0.1$, there is a less than (or equal to) 1 in 10 likelihood (10%) that the results were generated by chance (quite likely) – accept the null, may indicate trend obscured by poor method.

Which probability level to set?
- **usually**, $p \leq 0.05$ is acceptable for psychological research (see above) and the null will be rejected if this value or lower is obtained
- **sometimes more certainty is needed** (e.g. in medical matters) and then the null will not be rejected unless $p \leq 0.01$ or 0.001 is obtained
- also, **if the results of a study are opposite to previous findings**, a value of $p \leq 0.01$ is used.

> The lower the value of "p" set, the more stringent the test.

3.8 Ecological and experimental validity

Ecological validity
- **can you generalise** from the results or do they only apply in a particular situation?
- **if you cannot generalise** to real-life situations, the study lacks ecological validity
- **observation studies** tend to have high ecological validity.

Experimental validity
- see reliability and validity above (Section 2)
- **experiments are valid** if we can be relatively sure that any difference (or correlation) between data sets is due to the IV rather than extraneous variables
- **laboratory studies** with good control of extraneous variables result in high experimental validity.

Studies with high ecological validity usually lack experimental validity and vice versa.

Section 3

1. What is content analysis?

2. How should case studies be analysed?

3. What are measures of central tendency?

4. When is it appropriate to use the median?

5. List the measures of dispersion.

6. What are the main types of graphical representation?

7. When should a scattergraph be used?

8. List the statistical tests of difference.

9. Which difference tests can be used on related data?

10. When is it appropriate to use a Mann-Whitney U test?

11. What are the tests of correlation?

12. When is it appropriate to use Chi-square? – N.B. 2 instances.

13. What does a probability (p) value indicate?

14. What does $0.001 \leq p \leq 0.01$ mean?

15. What is the usual acceptable probability level for rejecting the null hypothesis?

16. What are ecological and experimental validity?

Index